MW00488641

The New
Brown Bag

Planting Seeds of Faith

 The New
Brown Bag

Planting Seeds of Faith

Virginia H. Loewen

THE
PILGRIM
PRESS
Cleveland

To the members of the former Saint John's United Methodist Church, who have dispersed to plant and nurture seeds of faith throughout the community of State College, Pennsylvania, and beyond.

The Pilgrim Press, 700 Prospect Avenue East
Cleveland, Ohio 44115-1100
pilgrimpress.com

© 2002 by Virginia H. Loewen

All rights reserved. Published 2002

Printed in the United States of America on acid-free paper

06 05 04 03 02   5 4 3 2 1

Library of Congress Cataloging-in-Publication Data

Loewen, Virginia H., 1932-
    Planting seeds of faith / Virginia H. Loewen.
        p.   cm.   (The new brown bag)
    Includes bibliographical references and index.
    ISBN 0-8298-1473-6 (alk. paper)
    1. Children's sermons.   I. Title.   II. Series

  BV4315 .L59   2002
  252'.53–dc21

                                                2002016961

Contents

Preface 7

Introduction 8

1. Special Names   Luke 1:31; Matthew 1:21 . 11

2. A Circle of Love   John 3:16 13

3. Joy! Joy! Joy!   Philippians 4:1, 4, 12–13 . 15

4. Did Jesus Have

      a Christmas Tree?   Hosea 14:8 18

5. Body Language   Matthew 2:11 21

6. Jesus Uses Signs   John 2:11 23

7. A Gift for Everyone   Ephesians 4:7–8, 11–12 . . . 26

8. Going Fishing   Matthew 4:19; Mark 1:17 . 28

9. A Valentine from God   Psalm 103:11–12 31

10. God Isn't Finished

      with Me Yet   Philippians 1:6 34

11. Pretzels and Prayers   Jeremiah 29:12 37

12. Are You Sleeping?   Matthew 26:41 41

13. The Greatest   Luke 22:26–27 44

14. The Eraser   Colossians 2:13–14 47

15. Messages   Matthew 28:7 50

16. Seeing and Believing   John 20:29 53

17. Treasures   Matthew 6:21; Luke 12:34   57

18. A Word with God   2 Timothy 3:16–17 60

19. In Tune with Jesus   Colossians 3:12–17 63

20. A Time for Growing   1 Corinthians 3:5–9 66

21. Playing Hide-and-Seek

     with God   Jeremiah 29:13–14 70

22. Crystal Clear   2 Corinthians 4:6 74

23. Claiming Territory   Psalm 89:11 77

24. Putting Things in Order   Genesis 1:1–2 80

25. God Knows Your Name   Isaiah 49:15b–16 84

26. Jesus Brings Good News   John 3:16 88

Bibliography 91

Index 93

Preface

As I continue my spiritual journey, I realize that we are most impressionable when we are children. What we learn—attitudes, habits, concepts, truth—stays with us through adulthood. Examples are a love of reading and an appreciation of fine music.

At this time and place in my journey, the Spirit is leading me to share what I have learned (and continue to learn) with children by teaching them. In Luke 18:15–17, we learn that Jesus welcomed little children because they have the kind of faith and trust needed to enter God's realm. It is important that we introduce our children to Jesus and that we, as adults, also approach him with childlike faith, acceptance, and trust.

From its beginning, *Planting Seeds of Faith* has been a group effort. Knowing that this is what I am to be writing, I also know that God will provide the inspiration and the energy to accomplish it. God has already provided help by speaking through many Christians, whom I want to thank for their support and encouragement. Among them are Norman Rohrer and Evelyn Minshull for their knowledgeable advice; the Christian Writers' Roundtable, especially Jean W. Sherman, Laurel West, and Emma Westerman, for many hours of inspired critiquing; the Rev. Dr. Ruth Ann Campagna and the Rev. Fred Hickok for field-testing sermons; Sojourners and the Gittings/Loewen ChristCare group from Saint Paul's United Methodist Church, State College, Pennsylvania; and others unnamed who supported this project and me with prayer. Most of all, thanks be to God for using me as an instrument of God's love.

Introduction

To each is given the manifestation of the Spirit for the common good.—1 Corinthians 12:7

Children are a vital factor in the growth formula of the Christian church. But attracting four- to eight-year-olds, holding their attention, and teaching them about God can be a daunting task. *Planting Seeds of Faith* is a nondenominational resource to aid pastors and laity who teach children in family worship services. An especially important part near the end of each message is the "take-away," an object or suggestion of a way to apply and share faith away from the church.

I pray that the following guidelines and tips will help the seeds that you plant produce a bountiful harvest. Praise the Holy Spirit for the gift of teaching!

Guidelines and Tips for *Planting Seeds of Faith*

❀ Carry props in a bag, basket, box, bucket, or any container appropriate for the topic or the season.

❀ Gather the children around you at the front of the sanctuary. Sit facing them on their level.

❀ Tell—don't read—the message. You may want to jot notes on a large index card or copy the lesson pages and keep them on your lap as you talk.

* Read scripture directly from your Bible, bookmarked with sticky notes. All scripture is quoted from the New Revised Standard Version.

* Use a lapel or portable microphone. If children's voices are not amplified, repeat their comments for the congregation.

* Make it fun and interesting. Be loving, but firm, if the children become too excited or noisy.

* Use language they understand.

* Pause for children to respond to questions and ideas.

* Expect logical answers from children but remember, also, to expect the unexpected. Be prepared for a few laughs—good medicine for the soul. Parentheses ( ) designate some possible answers. Assure the children when they give good answers.

* Add or substitute your own appropriate experiences or anecdotes. Asterisks (*) mark some opportunities to do this.

* Use the "take-away" to remind children of the lesson. It may be an object or a suggestion of a way to share faith away from the church—learning by doing.

* In children ages four through eight, understanding occurs at different levels. Include "Stretching Further" if more perceptive children need to be challenged. Use it as a part of the basic lesson or in a discussion that continues in a Sunday school class.

* Prayer: Ask the children to bow their heads and repeat your words. Pause between meaningful phrases while children pray aloud.

* Allow five to ten minutes for each lesson. Remember the short attention spans of young children. Adapt the message to the needs and interests of the children. Keep it focused and simple.

* Use most of the messages at any time of year. See the index for lessons for special days and "holydays."

1
Special Names

THEME: Names tell something special about us. The name "Jesus" means "Savior."

SCRIPTURE: You will name him Jesus.—Luke 1:31

You are to name him Jesus, for he will save his people from their sins.—Matthew 1:21

PREPARATION: Prepare to share an anecdote about how or why you or a friend received his or her name and nickname.

This is the season of the year that we call "Advent." The word "Advent" means that we are waiting for something to come. What we're waiting for will come after four Sundays. What are we waiting for? *(Christmas; the coming of Christ; celebrating the birthday of Jesus.)*

When a baby is born, the baby's parents choose a name for him or her. *(Use a personal or family example.)* Does anyone know why your parents gave you your name? *(Sometimes a boy is given the same name as his father or grandfather.)*

Sometimes people call us by our nicknames, especially if our name is a long word. *(Give a personal or family example.)* Do any of you have nicknames?

We can call ourselves other names, too. To your parents, you are their daughter or son. To your grandparents, you are their granddaughter or grandson. Someone else might call you friend.

Can you think of other names that you might be called? (*When you read, you are a reader; a writer, listener, speaker, runner, sleeper, musician, athlete, scout, student, helper.*)

Do you know why Jesus' mother gave him his name? (*An angel of the Lord told Mary, "You will name him Jesus" [Luke 1:31]. An angel told Joseph, also, to name him Jesus, "for he will save his people from their sins" [Matthew 1:21].*) The name "Jesus" means "Savior."

What other names for Jesus do we use when we talk or sing or read about him? (*Baby Jesus, carpenter, teacher, storyteller, healer, son of Mary, child of God, Good Shepherd, Lamb of God, comforter, counselor, Prince of Peace, King, deliverer of the Jews, Messiah, Jesus Christ, Christ Jesus, God, Emmanuel, friend.*)

Our names tell something special about us. There is another name that we call ourselves. If we believe in Jesus and that he is our Savior, we call ourselves believers (or Christians). And Advent is a very special time for believers in Jesus.

This week, when you write your name or someone calls you by your name, think about the name of Jesus and what he does for us.

OPTIONAL: STRETCHING FURTHER
What has Jesus done for us?

(*Join hands in a circle if the group is small.*) Will you bow your heads and pray by repeating after me? (*Say short, meaningful phrases.*)

Dear God, thank you for our special names. Thank you for the Baby Jesus and for helping us to become believers in Him. Help us to prepare to celebrate his birthday in this Advent season. We pray in Jesus' name. Amen.

2
A Circle of Love

THEME: God's love for us never ends.

SCRIPTURE: For God so loved the world that he gave his only Son, so that everyone who believes in him may not perish but may have eternal life.—John 3:16

PREPARATION: Gather an assortment of circular things such as food container lids, paper plates, empty ribbon spools, Styrofoam wreath forms, and embroidery hoops. Put them in a Christmas gift bag. In a second gift or grocery bag, place assorted foods shaped like circles or Os.

I have some things in this (*Christmas gift*) bag to show you. (*Give each child one thing, or let each child reach in and take out one item to hold.*) What do you have? Did you notice that there is something alike about all of these things? What shape are they? (*Round, circles.*)

Look at the circle you're holding. Can you tell where the circle begins? Where it ends? Why do you think I brought round things— circles—today? The circle reminds us of God's love for us. We can't tell where God's love begins, and we know it never ends. God always loves us. God loves us so much that God sent the baby Jesus to be born in Bethlehem, and Jesus loves us too.

Can you think of anything else that is shaped like a circle? (*Merry-go-round, hula-hoop, inner tubes, tires.*) Do you make circles when you draw or write? (*Letter O, numeral zero.*) Look around you. Do you see anything here that is round like a circle? (*Advent wreath, ornament O on a Christmas tree, round window, lamp shade.*) Am I wearing anything shaped like a circle? (*Wedding ring, circular or wreath pin, earrings.*)

Is there anything you like to eat that is shaped like a circle? (*If children need a visual cue, hold up one item at a time: *Cheerios™, Fruit Loops™, cookies, doughnuts, Spaghettios™, Lifesavers™.*)

These things can all remind us that God loves us and never stops loving us. We know that because the Bible tells us, "For God so loved the world that he gave his only Son,"—Jesus—"so that everyone who believes in him may not perish but may have eternal life" (John 3:16).

And Jesus tells us to love one another. What could we do with this food to show that we love people who don't have much to eat? (*Give it to a food bank or take it to someone's home.*)

This week, look for circles. Remember to thank God for your food. And, especially whenever you eat something that is shaped like a circle, thank God for loving us. God's love never ends.

OPTIONAL: STRETCHING FURTHER
Talk about Jesus our Savior—a true lifesaver.

Let's stand up and join hands and make a circle. We could make this circle even bigger. How? If you know someone who doesn't go to church or Sunday school, you could invite that person to come with you to learn how much God loves all of us.

Let's pray. (*Ask children to bow their heads and repeat after you. Say short, meaningful phrases.*)

Dear God, we thank you for loving us. We know that your love for us never ends, and nothing can stop you from loving us. We thank you for Jesus, and we pray in his name. Amen.

(*Have an older child or two put the bag of food in the food bank container.*)

3
Joy! Joy! Joy!

THEME: Joy is knowing that we have Jesus, the best gift of all.

SCRIPTURE: Therefore, my brothers and sisters, whom I love and long for, my joy and my crown, stand firm in the Lord in this way. . . . Rejoice in the Lord always; again I will say, Rejoice. . . . In any and all circumstances I have learned the secret of being well fed and of going hungry, of having plenty and of being in need. I can do all things through him who strengthens me.—Philippians 4:1, 4, 12–13

PREPARATION: Cut enough rectangles, about 3 1/2" x 1 1/2", from colored paper to give one or two to each child. Draw a bow on each paper "present." Be joyful!

Are you excited that Christmas will soon be here? Is there a special gift that you want most of all to receive? How will you feel if you get that special thing? How will you feel if you don't get that one special thing? Will you still be happy?

There are some letters in the Bible written by a man named Paul. Paul had been arrested and put in prison—jail—even though he had not been found guilty of breaking any law. While he was in prison, he wrote letters to the people—the church—in a place called Philippi. Do you think Paul was happy to be in jail for something he didn't do?

In his letters, he wrote about a secret that he had learned: "I know what it is to have little, and I know what it is to have plenty. In any and all circumstances I have learned the secret of being well-fed and of going hungry, of having plenty and of being in need" (Philippians 4:12). Can you imagine being happy even when something bad or sad happens? Paul wrote that he had learned to be happy even when he didn't have all the things he needed and even when he didn't have enough to eat. Have you ever been hungry or thirsty? cold? sick? alone? hurt? Were you happy then?

What do you think Paul's secret was? How could he be happy even in bad times? He wrote, "I can do all things through him who strengthens me" (Philippians 4:13). Paul thought about what God wanted him to *do*, not what Paul wanted to *have*. He believed that Jesus Christ gave him strength to face any troubles or problems he might have.

Paul wrote to the people in Philippi: "Rejoice in the Lord always" (Philippians 4:4). He thanked them, too, for the gifts they had sent to him in prison. They had found joy in giving, as he had found joy in receiving. He believed that Jesus Christ gave him strength to face any troubles or problems he might have.

This is a time of year when people like to keep secrets, especially about Christmas presents. I am going to ask you to keep a special secret. First, I want you to think about one gift that you could give to someone you love, not a gift that you could buy, but a promise to *do* something for that special person. (*Encourage suggestions from the children. Suggest drawing a picture of yourself or your family; writing a story; promising to make your bed and put your toys away when you're done playing with them; helping to set the table; when guests arrive, taking care of their coats; helping to gather the wrapping paper and ribbons after packages have been opened; sharing your toys and gifts with brothers and sisters; reading a story to a brother or sister who hasn't learned to read yet.*)

*Something that gives me joy is hearing my grandson singing at home the songs he learns at church or Sunday school. On Easter Sunday he sang, "God's not dead! *No!* God is alive. God's not dead! *No!* God is alive." Maybe you have another idea of what you could do to make someone joyful. But don't tell me, and don't tell that special person what you are going to do. Keep the secret.

Now I am going to give each of you a piece (or two pieces) of colored paper that looks (or look) like a Christmas present. Before Christmas Day is here, decide what you will do as a gift for someone (or two people) who is (or are) very important to you. If you can, write your promise on the back of the package. On Christmas Day, give these "presents" to your Mom, Dad, brother, sister, grandma, grandpa, or a good friend, and tell them what you will *do* for them as a gift to bring them joy.

The feeling that you get when you *give* a gift or *do* something for someone else is the warm, wonderfully happy feeling of joy. Joy is more than a Christmas tree, more than pretty decorations and lights, more than presents wrapped in bright-colored paper, more than cookies and parties. Joy is knowing that we have Jesus, the best gift of all.

OPTIONAL: STRETCHING FURTHER

Consider Psalm 28:7: "My heart exults, and with my song I give thanks to him." David wrote that his heart jumps for joy. He is so happy that he wants to say thank you to God with a song. What songs do we sing that have the word joy or joyful, joyous or rejoice in them? (*"Down in My Heart"*; *"Joy to the World"*; *"Joyful, Joyful, We Adore Thee"*; *"Good Christian Men Rejoice"*; *"God Rest Ye Merry, Gentlemen"*; *"While Shepherds Watched Their Flocks"*; *"O, Come, All Ye Faithful"*; *"Hark the Herald Angels Sing."*) With the congregation, have the children sing one of these songs as they return to their seats.

Let's pray. (*Ask children to bow their heads and repeat after you. Say short, meaningful phrases.*)

Dear God, we thank you for the good news of great joy that the angels brought long ago. Thank you for our brother Jesus. He teaches us how to love one another. Help us to be filled with joy because Jesus is the best gift of all. In his name we pray. Amen.

4
Did Jesus Have a Christmas Tree?

THEME: We can count on God to be our friend and helper through all the seasons (all the time).

SCRIPTURE: O, Ephraim, what have I to do with idols? It is I who answer and look after you. I am like an evergreen cypress; your faithfulness comes from me.—Hosea 14:8

PREPARATION: Bring a fresh evergreen branch of cedar, pine, or another fragrant tree.

Are you getting ready to celebrate Jesus' birthday at your house? at your school or child care center? If I came to your home or your school, what would I see, or hear, or smell that tells me you're getting ready for Christmas? (*Drawings and stories about Santa and his reindeer, red and green paper chains, ornaments, tinsel, holly, a tree, cookies, Christmas cards, Christmas songs, packages, wrapping paper, wreaths.*)

We know that on the very first Christmas there ever was, Jesus was born to Mary and Joseph. Did Jesus have a Christmas tree? as a baby? as a teenager? Why not?

Do you know how Christmas trees became a part of our celebration? Long, long ago, people thought that a god lived inside a tree. When the wind blew through leaves on the branches, the leaves rubbed against each other and made a kind of whispering sound. The people thought it was the god inside the tree talking.

But in winter, there were no leaves left on those trees. People noticed that trees with leaves shaped like needles stayed green all year long. They wanted to bring something of the beautiful world of nature indoors, and so they cut branches from the evergreen trees. Sometimes they made garlands (wreaths) from the greens.

Early Christians did not bring evergreens indoors. But as hundreds of years passed, no one believed anymore that a god of nature lived inside trees. Then Christians, too, decorated their homes with evergreen trees.

In Germany, people brought fruit trees indoors so they would bloom in winter. Others who believed that Christmas was a magical time when many trees bloomed decorated evergreen trees with roses cut from colored paper and with apples and sweet things to eat. The idea of decorating a tree at Christmastime spread from Germany to England and then to America.

Is there anything about a Christmas tree that makes you think of Jesus? (*Star: the star of Bethlehem; angels: announced that Jesus was born; lights: Jesus said, "I am the light of the world" [John 8:12]; bells: ringing, celebrating good news; the tree itself: created by God and Jesus; fragrance: Mary, sister of Martha and Lazarus, poured perfume on Jesus' feet. [John 12:3]*)

There is a way that God is like an evergreen tree. About seven hundred years before Jesus was born, a man named Hosea told the people of Israel that God said they should have nothing to do with idols. That means don't worship statues or a god you think lives in a tree. God said, "It is I who answer and look after you. I am like an evergreen cypress: your faithfulness comes from me" (Hosea 14:8b). That means your blessings, the good things, come from God. We can count on God to be our friend and helper all the time, not just in one season of the year.

We can find reminders of Jesus and God the Parent even in a Christmas tree or a wreath. If you help to decorate a tree, share what you learned about Christmas trees. But, more important than that, share the good news, the story the angels brought about Jesus. Ask your friends or family, "Do you know why there is a star or an angel on the top of the tree?"

OPTIONAL: STRETCHING FURTHER

Read aloud Hosea 14:6–7. Talk about how God compares people to trees. (*The people will be like spreading branches. They will be like the beautiful olive trees. They will be like sweet-smelling cedars in Lebanon. The people of Israel will again live under my protection. They will grow like grain. They will bloom like a vine.*)

Let's pray. (*Ask children to bow their heads and repeat after you. Say short, meaningful phrases.*)

Dear God, as we get ready to celebrate Christmas, help us to remember Jesus. Thank you for watching over us through all the seasons of the year. We pray in the name of your son, Jesus. Amen.

5
Body Language

THEME: When we kneel or bow our heads to pray, we show honor and respect to God.

SCRIPTURE: They [the wise men] saw the child with Mary his mother; and they knelt down and paid him homage.
—Matthew 2:11

PREPARATION: Recall an anecdote about yourself, an athlete, a family member, or friend about knee(s), such as exercises, injury, surgery, or a "trick knee." You may wish to substitute your story for the author's example.* A crèche or a picture of the wise men kneeling before Jesus will be helpful. You may want to use a small chalkboard, marker board, or a large paper tablet to print "knee." Then add "l" to spell "kneel."

Today we are going to talk about knees. Let's all touch our knees. Are knees an important part of your body? Why? (*Without knee joints, our legs wouldn't bend.*) What do your knees let you do? (*Walk, run, jump, swim, climb, ride a tricycle or bicycle.*) Sometimes a doctor checks to see how you're doing by taking a little hammer and tapping your leg below your kneecap. What happens to your leg when the doctor does that? (*It jerks upward involuntarily.*)

Knees can be tricky. Sometimes they make noises, especially when we grow old.

*I have a brother whose knees made a crunching sound, even when he was a teenager. I always knew when he climbed the stairs, especially late at night.

Does anyone know how to spell the word "knee"? It's a tricky word. We don't hear the first letter at all. (*Name the letters as you print them.*) If we add one more letter to the end of "knee," we can spell the word "kneel." Who knows how to spell "kneel"? Let's say the word "kneel" together, spell it, and say it again: "kneel," "k-n-e-e-l," "kneel." Now pat your knees gently with your hands while we spell it again. Good!

Could you kneel without bending your legs at the knee? When do you kneel? Why do we sometimes kneel to pray?

Kneeling is a way that we can use our bodies to show how we feel. We call that "body language." When you salute the flag, how do you use your body to show that you respect the flag? (*Put your hand over your heart.*) When someone in a military uniform meets an officer, what does the lower-ranking person do? (*Demonstrate a salute.*)

When the wise men came from far away and saw the baby Jesus with his mother Mary, they bowed down and worshiped him. They believed that this child was going to be the king, and they bowed down or kneeled to show him respect, to honor him, and to worship him.

When we bow our heads or kneel to pray, we mean that we are not our own bosses; God is the one we obey; God is our ruler. If someone isn't able to kneel, that person can still show respect and honor by bowing the head.

Maybe some of you already kneel to say your bedtime prayers. If you are not in the habit of kneeling, remember to do that tonight. Remember that kneeling says to God, "I love you. I honor you. I respect you." You might want to kneel every night to talk to God.

OPTIONAL: STRETCHING FURTHER
Read aloud and talk about Philippians 2:10: "At the name of Jesus every knee should bend, in heaven and on earth and under the earth."

Let's all bend our knees and kneel to pray to God today:

Dear God, we thank you for our knees. They let us walk and run and jump. They let us kneel to show that you are our God and king. Help us to obey you. We pray in the name of Jesus. Amen.

6
Jesus Uses Signs

THEME: Jesus' miracles were signs that he is the child of God.

SCRIPTURE: Jesus did this, the first of his signs, in Cana of Galilee, and revealed his glory; and his disciples believed in him.—John 2:11

PREPARATION: Observe the colors, shapes, words, and so forth, on various signs inside the church building and outside, in the neighborhood, where the church is located.

Today we're going to talk about signs. Did you see any signs along the way to church today? What kind of signs did you see? (*Elicit responses from children, giving clues as needed. Example: I saw a sign that had eight sides. It was red. Across the middle of it were some white letters: "S-T-O-P." So every time I see a sign like that, I know I must do what? Yes, stop my car or bicycle, or even stop walking and look carefully before I go on.*)

What other kinds of signs have you seen? (*Street names, no parking, neighborhood or project signs, church name signs, exit, restroom, name tags.*) Most of the signs we've been talking about have letters on them for us to read. But there are signs around us that tell us something without letters. When a traffic light turns green, it tells me to do what? (*Go.*) When I see the sky covered with dark clouds in winter, I know *what* might happen? (*It might snow.*) When I see lightning in summer, what do I know? (*Thunder will follow; a storm is coming; it's going to rain.*) When the sun sinks below the edge of the earth, that's a sign that *what* is going to happen? (*It's getting dark; night is coming.*)

Did you know that Jesus used signs? Not the kinds of signs we've been talking about. Jesus' signs are called miracles. We read in the Bible, "Jesus did . . . the first of his signs, in Cana of Galilee, and revealed his glory; and his disciples believed in him" (John 2:11).

Do you know what the first miracle is that Jesus did? Jesus had gone to a party after two of his friends got married. We would call that kind of party a wedding reception. At that time, wedding parties lasted a whole week. Often the whole town was invited, and if someone didn't come, it was very bad manners. For the whole town to celebrate for a whole week meant that the person giving the party had to provide lots of food and a lot to drink.

Now think with me about the kinds of fruit juices we like to drink. Have you ever been to a place like Florida or California where oranges grow on trees? When you live where oranges grow, you can enjoy drinking orange juice at every meal if you want to do that. There are apple orchards near where we live. Who likes to drink apple juice or cider? Galilee, where Jesus was attending a wedding party, was a place where grapes grew well. So the people drank wine, made from grape juice. They added a lot of water to the wine so it wasn't very strong, and they drank it at every meal.

Can you imagine how embarrassing it would be if you had a party and you didn't have enough for everyone to drink? That's what happened at the wedding reception in the town called Cana of Galilee. Jesus' mother, Mary, told him that their friends had run out of wine. Then Jesus told the servants to fill the jars with water. They held more than 120 gallons. When the guests tasted what was in the jars, it was the best wine that was served at the party. Jesus had performed a miracle.

What is a miracle? (*A totally unexpected happening or event that shows God's special power at work.*) Do you know any other miracles that Jesus performed? (*Made a blind man see; made a lame person walk; made a deaf man hear; brought dead persons back to life; calmed the winds and the waves in a storm; fed 5,000 people by blessing five loaves and two fishes.*)

Why do you think Jesus did those miracles? Yes, he wanted to help people whose bodies weren't working the way they should. He wanted to make them well, and he wanted to give food to people who were hungry. He did miracles for another reason, too. In the Bible, John calls Jesus' miracles "signs." The miracles were signs that Jesus is the child of God. Because he is the child of God, he is more powerful than all the laws of nature. He is *Almighty God*; there is nothing he can't do!

Jesus lived on Earth many years ago. We have not seen him doing those miracles. But we have the Bible—a record of his miracles. Jesus said that some people wouldn't believe that he was, and is, the child of God unless they saw him do "signs and wonders" (John 4:48). But, "Blessed are those who have not seen and yet have come to believe" (John 20:29).

Look for signs on your way home, on your way to school, inside your school, and on your playground this week. Whenever you see a sign, pay attention to what it says. But remember, too, the signs that Jesus gave us, the miracles he did so that people might believe he is the child of God.

OPTIONAL: STRETCHING FURTHER
Talk about the miracle at the wedding in Cana as an example or sign of the way Jesus would go about his ministry: helping others, speaking with authority, and being in personal touch with people.

Let's pray. (*Ask children to bow their heads and repeat after you. Say short, meaningful phrases.*)

Dear God, we thank you for signs. Help us to follow signs that will keep us safe. Thank you for the miracles that Jesus did as signs to show that he is your child. We know that you love us. Help us to look for signs of your love and help us to be more loving to others. We pray in Jesus' name. Amen.

7
A Gift for Everyone

THEME: God (Christ) gave each of us a special gift.

SCRIPTURE: But each of us was given grace according to the measure of Christ's gift. Therefore . . . he gave gifts to his people.—Ephesians 4:7–8

The gifts he gave were that some would be apostles, some prophets, some evangelists, some pastors and teachers, to equip the saints for the work of ministry, for building up the body of Christ.—Ephesians 4:11–12

PREPARATION: Use a variety of colored construction paper or index cards to cut rectangles about 5" x 1 1/2". With a marker, print on each card a spiritual gift, such as telling the good news (apostles); telling God's message (prophesy); teaching; doing miracles; healing; helping others; being a leader; speaking in different languages; telling what different languages mean; caring for God's people; serving; encouraging; giving; showing mercy; hospitality. Put the cards in a decorative box with a lift-off lid. Place a gift bow on top.

Is there anyone here who likes to get presents? Does this box look like it could be a present? There's another word that we use for something that someone gives us—"gift."

Do you think this box is big enough to hold a gift for every one of you? for all the grownups who are here today? for the whole world?

In the Bible, we can read a letter that Paul wrote to the people at a place called Ephesus. Paul wrote that Christ gave each one of us a special gift (Ephesians 4:7). *Note: For small children, you may want to substitute "God" for "Christ."*

But the kinds of gifts that come from God are not the kinds of gifts you might get on Christmas or on your birthday. The gifts we read about in Paul's letter to the Ephesians are called gifts of the Spirit, or spiritual gifts. I hope that what is in this box will help us to see the kinds of gifts we're talking about today. (*Ask a child to take off the lid and take out one card. If the child can't read the card, read it aloud for him or her. Continue having cards drawn and read as time permits.*)

These are *some* of the gifts that God gives. There are more gifts that we haven't mentioned today. But each one of us has been given at least one gift from the Spirit of God.

God didn't give everyone the *same* gift. Do you know why? It's like our bodies. Suppose our bodies were just one great big ear! How would we see or walk and talk? Or, suppose our bodies were just one big eye. That wouldn't work at all! So God gave different gifts for all of us to work together, each one using his special gift to make the church strong.

You might not know what your special gift is. As you grow up, part of your work will be to find out what gift(s) God gave you. We can help each other to discover our special gifts. Our friends, our pastors, and our parents can help us. You might want to ask your parents if they know what *their* spiritual gifts are. And we can ask God to show us what *our* gifts are. And guess what! When you discover what your gifts are and start using them to do the kind of work God wants you to do, it will be so much fun—the best time of your whole life!

Did you notice that the cards inside the box were of different colors? This week, when you use colored paper, markers, crayons, or paints, let those colors remind you that you have a special gift from God. If you ask God, God will help you to find it.

OPTIONAL: STRETCHING FURTHER
Continue drawing cards from the gift box. Comment on those that may need explanation. If time permits, refer to Romans 12:6–8 or 1 Corinthians 12:27–31 for more about spiritual gifts.

Let's pray. (*Ask children to bow their heads and repeat after you. Say short, meaningful phrases.*)

Dear God, thank you for making us all different. Help us to find the gifts you've given to every one of us. Help us to use those gifts to help the church grow strong and to be your body in the world. We pray in Jesus' name. Amen.

8
Going Fishing

THEME: When we follow Jesus, we can attract others to him, too.

SCRIPTURE: And he said to them, "Follow me, and I will make you fish for people."—Matthew 4:19; Mark 1:17 (*Note that earlier translations say "fishers of men."*)

PREPARATION: Gather clothes and fishing equipment, such as a rod, reel, line, bobber, bait or lure, and net. (Or invite someone who fishes to participate with you in presenting the children's message.) *Note: For safety, don't bring hooks. For "Stretching Further," notice where in the church building the symbol of a fish is used. You may want to gather items such as a lapel pin, bookmark, auto emblem, poster, bulletin, or necktie to show to the children.*

How do you like my outfit this morning? Do I look like I'm ready for church? No? What do you think I'm ready to do? Yes, I've been thinking about going fishing. Have you ever gone fishing? I wonder if I have everything I need.

I'm really not going fishing right now. First of all, since this is Sunday, I've come to church. I know that one thing we will do here is read or listen to the Bible.

I'm looking at the part of the Bible that tells about Jesus and what he did. Do you think I can find anything here about fish or fishing?

Do you know that Jesus did miracles with fish? (*Encourage knowledgeable children to tell about the miracles.*) In the book of Matthew (14:17–21), we read about a big crowd of people who came to hear Jesus and to see him heal those who were sick. There were more than 5,000 people, and they were hungry. Jesus had only *five loaves of bread and two fish.* He looked up to heaven, thanked God for the fish and bread, and then broke the loaves. The disciples gave the food to the people. After they had all eaten and were full, there were still twelve basketfuls of pieces left over!

Do you like to eat fish? In the time and place where Jesus lived, fish was a common food. The Sea of Galilee was really a lake with the Jordan River running through it. Many different kinds of fish lived in that lake. So, instead of meat and potatoes, or chicken and rice, as some of us might eat, they ate fish and bread.

The people, usually the men, who lived near the Sea of Galilee made a living by catching fish and selling them. They caught the fish by throwing out a big net and then pulling it back in toward the boat. Sometimes the net would tear. So they would have to mend the net before they threw it out again.

One day Jesus was walking along the shore of the Sea of Galilee. He saw two brothers—Simon and Andrew—throwing a net into the lake to catch fish: "And he said to them, 'Follow me, and I will make you fish for people.' Immediately they left their nets and followed him. As he went from there, he saw two other brothers, James son of Zebedee and his brother John, in the boat with their father Zebedee, mending their nets, and he called them. Immediately they left the boat and their father, and followed him" (Matthew 4:18–22).

Simon, Andrew, James, and John went with Jesus for a while, and then they went back to fishing. One day, when the people again crowded around Jesus, he got into Simon's boat and told him to go "out a little way from the shore. Then he sat down and taught the crowds from the boat. When he had finished speaking, he said to Simon, 'Put out into the deep water and let down your nets for a catch.' Simon answered, 'Master, we have worked all night long but have caught nothing. Yet if you say so, I will let down the nets.' When they had done this, they caught so many fish that their nets were beginning to break. So they signaled their partners in the other boat to come and help them. And they came and filled both boats, so that they began to sink." They were all amazed, and Simon was afraid. "Then Jesus said to Simon, 'Do not be afraid; from now on you will be catching people.'" (*Repeat for emphasis: "from now on you will be catching people!"*) "When they had brought their boats to shore, they left everything and followed him" (Luke 5:1–11).

Many people had seen and heard Jesus, but Simon, Andrew, James, and John did more than just watch and listen. They left their work, gave up the way they earned a living, and went with Jesus. They followed him and became his disciples. They began to "fish" for other people who might become his disciples, too.

Jesus needed those men to help, to go with him as he taught about God, and healed, and did good things for people. Jesus wants *us* to follow him, too. How can we follow him today? By living as he lived, being like him in what we do, praying, and letting him be our leader when we need to decide hard things, we are following Jesus.

And when people see that we are kind and loving, sharing, helpful, and happy, even when bad things happen, they will want to know how and why we can feel that way. When we tell them about our good friend, Jesus, they will want to know him, too. Then, we are like fishers who "catch" people and bring them in for God.

Do you think you might actually go fishing soon? Do you think you might eat fish next week? If you do, or even if you don't, remember that Jesus wants us to follow him, be like him, and love one another. By being loving and kind and by telling others about Jesus, we can be fishers, too, catching people for God.

OPTIONAL: STRETCHING FURTHER

Talk about the meaning of the fish as a symbol of Christianity. It reminded early Christians of the loaves and fishes and of Jesus' promise to make the disciples fishers of people. The letters of the Greek word for fish—*ichthus*—form an acronym for "Jesus Christ, God's Son, Savior." During times of persecution, early Christians could identify themselves to one another by drawing the sign of the fish. The fish sign also stood for baptism in living water. Even today, the sign or symbol of a fish on someone's car means that person is a Christian.

Let's pray. (*Ask children to bow their heads and repeat after you. Say short, meaningful phrases.*)

Dear God, thank you for your child, Jesus. He is our good friend. Help us to be like him. Help us to tell others about him. We pray in Jesus' name. Amen.

9

A Valentine from God

THEME: The Bible is a love letter from God to us.

SCRIPTURE: For as the heavens are high above the earth, so great is his steadfast love toward those who fear him; as far as the east is from the west, so far he removes our transgressions from us.—Psalm 103:11–12

PREPARATION: Gather a varied assortment of valentines. Cut enough 3" x 5" index cards in half for one piece per child. Place a heart-shaped sticker on each 3" x 2 1/2" card.

Are you excited about Valentine's Day? Do you know how Valentine's Day began? There are several different legends. In all of the stories, there is a man named Valentine. He was a Roman priest or bishop in the third century, about 269 C.E. He was sent to jail because he helped the Christians and disobeyed Emperor Claudius. One story says that he became a friend of the jail-keeper's daughter and cured her blindness. On the day that he was put to death, he wrote her a note, signed, "Your Valentine."

It had been the custom in Rome to celebrate a love festival on February 15 in honor of a goddess named Juno. During the festival, called *Lupercalia*, girls' names were put into a jar, and boys chose their partners by drawing names from it. The young people exchanged gifts and, later on, some of them married their partners.

In the fifth century (496 C.E.), the leaders of the Christian church in Rome wanted to get rid of the customs of *Lupercalia* that had nothing to do with God in the Bible. So they chose February 14 to honor Saint Valentine instead. Through hundreds of years,

Valentine's Day has become a special day for people to give gifts, write poems, and send messages that say "I like you" or "I love you." (*Show and talk about the valentines you brought and how each one is different.*)

I remember some valentines that I received long ago. I remember the first, pretty valentine that I got from a boy in the fifth grade. It had a drawing of a sugar bowl and sugar cubes and the words said something about being as sweet as sugar.

In the tenth grade, someone gave me a big, red, heart-shaped box of chocolate candy on Valentine's Day. That was extra special! But the most special valentine of all is the one my husband gave me this year. The words say: "I love you more each year."

Would you believe me if I said I have a valentine from God? What would a valentine from God look like? Would it be shaped like a heart? Why? (*A heart stands for love, and God loves us.*) Might it be shaped like a cross, or have a cross on it? Why? (*Jesus died on a cross.*)

A valentine from God would say, "See how much I love you." The Bible does that. It's like a letter addressed to each of you, "Dear (*name*)," and signed, "Jehovah God." When we read the Bible or listen to someone reading it, we can hear God telling us in many ways, "I love you. I will always love you." We read in the book of John, "For God so loved the world that he gave his only Son, so that everyone who believes in him may not perish but may have eternal life" (John 3:16).

In Psalms we read, "For as the heavens are high above the earth, so great is his steadfast love toward those who fear him; as far as the east is from the west, so far he removes our transgressions from us" (Psalm 103:11–12). That's how much God loves us, as high as the sky is above the earth. (*Extend arms and raise hands toward the sky; ask the children to do the same.*) And God says that if you're sorry when you've done bad things, I will take those bad things as far away as the east (*lower one arm; point eastward*) is from the west (*extend other arm westward*). I'll take them so far away that they will never meet. I'll forgive you and I won't even remember what you've done.

How can you send a valentine back to God? (*Praise, thank, or sing a song to God; forgive those who don't treat you kindly; love one another.*) Jesus said, "Love the Lord your God with all your heart, and with all your soul, and with all your mind, and with all your strength. . . .

Love your neighbor as yourself" (Mark 12:30–31). And Jesus said, "They who have my commandments and keep them are those who love me" (John 14:21). So when we love God and obey God, that is like sending a valentine—a love letter—back to God.

I'm going to give each of you a card with a heart sticker on it. Carry it in your pocket or take it home and put it someplace where you will see it often this week. You could use it as a bookmark in your Bible or Bible storybook. Every time you see or feel the card, remember that the Bible is like a valentine from God. And if you see or meet someone who is feeling sad or having a bad day, give your card to that person and say, "God loves you."

OPTIONAL: STRETCHING FURTHER

The apostle Paul wrote, "You yourselves are our letter, written on our hearts to be known and read by all" (2 Corinthians 3:2). How can *we* be *letters* (valentines) from Jesus Christ to other people?

Let's pray. (*Ask children to bow their heads and repeat after you. Say short, meaningful phrases.*)

Thank you, God, for loving us. Thank you for the Bible. It tells how much you love us. Help us to love someone who needs a friend. We pray in Jesus' name. Amen.

10
God Isn't Finished with Me Yet

THEME: God works in us throughout our lifetime to make us more like Jesus in all we do and say.

SCRIPTURE: I am confident of this, that the one who began a good work among you will bring it to completion by the day of Jesus Christ.—Philippians 1:6

PREPARATION: Bring one or two wooden spoons (preferably a new one and an old, used one). Cut sandpaper into 2- or 3-inch squares or rectangles to provide one per child.

I brought something to show you today. (*Show one spoon.*) Do you know what this is? How do you think I use this spoon? I use this spoon for mixing good things to eat, like brownies.

I brought another spoon to show you, too. Are these two spoons alike? How are they alike? (*They're made of wood, have long round handles and slightly bowl-shaped ends.*) How are they different? (*The older, used spoon looks darker and feels somewhat smoother than the new one.*) Why do you think the older spoon looks different from the new one? (*Much stirring and mixing of foods have made the bowl end smoother. Dark-colored foods, like chocolate brownie batter, have stained the wood.*)

Why do you think I brought these wooden spoons today? Do you know anyone in the Bible who made things from wood? (*Joseph and Jesus.*) What do we call someone who works with wood? (*A carpenter.*) We know that Joseph was a carpenter, and he taught Jesus how to work with wood, too. When Jesus was growing up, he lived with his family in the village of Nazareth (Matthew 13:54–57; Mark 6:1–4). We think that Jesus might have worked for twenty years as a carpenter before he left his home there.

Joseph made wooden things for the village people to use. Do you think he might have made wooden spoons? He might have made wooden dishes, too. Can you think of other things Joseph and Jesus might have made for people to use inside their houses? *(Benches, tables, chairs, boxes.)* Joseph made tools for farmers to use, too, like plows, yokes to put over animals' necks, handles for tools, and carts with wooden wheels.

Now imagine a farmer coming to Joseph's carpenter shop, long ago, saying, "I need a new cart for my donkey to pull. If you make it for me, I'll come back to get it when it's finished."

So imagine Joseph and Jesus working together to make the cart. Every few days the farmer came to the shop and asked, "Is my cart finished yet?" But Joseph and Jesus wanted to do their work well and make the cart strong and sturdy so the farmer could use it for many years.

The farmer came back again and again, but the cart still wasn't finished.

At last, Joseph and Jesus were ready to make the wheels for the cart. By and by, they had made three round cartwheels, but the fourth one wasn't perfectly round. When they pushed the cart over the ground, it bumped along instead of turning smoothly.

That day the farmer came back and saw the cart sitting there with four wheels on it. "At last," he said, "I will pay you for my cart and take it with me."

Joseph said, "No, it isn't finished yet. You can't take it."

"Of course it's finished. And it's mine," said the farmer. "I'm going to take it."

What do you think happened next? Would the farmer be happy?

This story about Joseph and Jesus is not a story you will find in the Bible. It came from my imagination. I believe that Joseph was an honest man who worked hard and finished the work he began.

God is like that. When God starts a project, God finishes it. We are God's projects. God began working in us when we first believed in God and wanted to be more like Jesus.

But we're different from things made of wood. A cart or a spoon can't think or talk. It can't say, "I want to be smooth or round or shiny."

But we *can* think and talk, and sometimes we do or say things that hurt other people or make them sad. We can say, "I'm sorry I did that," or "I'm sorry I said that," or "I'm sorry that I took something that wasn't mine," or "I'm sorry I disobeyed you, Mom or Dad."

When we are sorry, Jesus the carpenter helps to make us better people. When we ask him, he helps us get rid of those bad ideas, and make a habit of saying kind words, and telling the truth.

Just as the spoon has changed, we change as we let God use us. God works with us when we are children, young people, and older people to smooth our rough edges and make us the best that we can be with Jesus as our example to follow.

God isn't finished with you or me yet. Do you think God is finished with any of these people here today? Paul writes in a letter to the people at Philippi, "I am confident of this, that the one who began a good work among you will bring it to completion by the day of Jesus Christ" (Philippians 1:6). He means that God began doing a good work in you. And God will continue until it is finished when Jesus Christ comes again. And God always keeps promises.

I'm going to give each of you a little piece of a special kind of paper. It's called sandpaper because one side is covered with sand. Do you know how sandpaper is used? Sandpaper is something a carpenter or woodworker might use, rubbing it back and forth over rough wood to make it smooth. (Demonstrate.) Isn't it strange that something that feels so rough can make what it's used on feel smooth—the opposite of rough? (Joseph and Jesus would have used a lump of sandstone to make things smooth.) I would like you to put this piece of sandpaper in your pocket and carry it with you this week as a reminder that God isn't finished with us yet. And God can even use our saddest times to make us grow to become more like Jesus in what we do and say.

OPTIONAL: STRETCHING FURTHER

Talk about our part in "finishing" us. (Learning about Jesus and how he wants us to live.) How can we do that? (By studying the Bible, coming to Sunday school and church, praying for help wherever we are.)

Let's pray: (Ask children to bow their heads and repeat after you. Say short, meaningful phrases.)

Dear God, thank you for Jesus and the good work that he does. Help us to practice being more like him. Help us to be sorry when we have made someone sad. We are glad that you are not finished with us yet. Amen.

11
Pretzels and Prayers

THEME: God always hears us—whenever, wherever, and however we pray.

SCRIPTURE: When you call upon me and come and pray to me, I will hear you.—Jeremiah 29:12

PREPARATION: Obtain the largest pretzel available, perhaps a soft pretzel sold by a vendor or from the frozen foods section of a supermarket. If suitable, after the prayer, treat the children to small pretzels or large ones cut or broken into small pieces.

I brought a BIG pretzel to show you today. Do you have any idea why I brought a pretzel to church? Pretzels were first made by believers in Jesus Christ. What do we call believers in Jesus Christ? Christians!

The Christians long ago had begun to "fast" during the forty days before they celebrated Easter. Who knows what "fasting" means? "Fasting" is giving up certain foods for a while. People sometimes fast during a special time of prayer and worship. Jesus himself fasted for forty days and forty nights before he began preaching (Matthew 4:2).

Who knows what we call the forty days before Easter? We call that season before Easter "Lent." During Lent, the Christians who fasted didn't eat fat, eggs, or milk. So they made a special bread dough that had only flour, salt, and water in it. They formed the dough into a long roll. Then they shaped it to look like two arms crossed in prayer. (*Demonstrate and ask the children to cross their arms, putting their hands on their shoulders.*) Look at someone else. Can you imagine that the arms form an X, or a cross? The crossed arms on the pretzel reminded the Christians that Lent is a time to think about Jesus, to pray, and to be sorry for the wrong things they knew they had done. They called these breads "little arms"—*bracellae* in the Latin language. The German people also made these "little arms" and called them *brezel* or *prezel*, from which we get our word "pretzel."

The early Christians in most of the countries of Europe made and ate pretzels only during Lent when they were fasting. Special people—*brezelmann*—sold them on Ash Wednesday on the streets. People ate them for lunch. Sometimes they ate pretzels in soup. In the country of Austria, the children carried palm branches hung with pretzels on Palm Sunday. It became the custom for the men and boys coming home from their Easter church service—confession—to decorate their hats with flowers and to give pretzels to everyone in the house. After Easter, pretzels wouldn't be seen again until the next Lenten season.

It was only in modern times that pretzels became snacks for us to nibble on anytime. Most people have forgotten what pretzels meant to Christians during Lent. After church, ask your parents if they know about pretzels. I hope that pretzels will remind all of us to pray.

I don't think I know anyone who crosses arms to pray, as we see in the pretzel. Do you? So what should we do with our bodies when we pray? There are many ways that people can show that they are praying—talking—to God. Some people might make the sign of the cross by touching their forehead and chest. Must we always close our eyes? fold our hands? Should we sit, stand, or kneel? Some people pray with their eyes open and their hands lifted toward heaven. Someone else might lie down with his face toward the earth to pray. Most of us pray in the way that our family and the people in our church are in the habit of doing. There is no "magic" in the position we choose for praying, or in what we do with our hands and eyes. What is more important is that we concentrate on talking to God. We need to focus on God with our hearts, our thoughts, and our feelings. Many people find that bowing their heads, closing their eyes, and folding their hands help them to do that.

Does anyone here like to talk? Do you have a friend or someone in your family with whom you talk a lot? You might tell that person about the happy, fun, exciting things that are happening. Might you also talk to that friend when you are sad and unhappy or when you have a problem? God is a friend like that. God wants to hear from you. In the Bible, we read God's Word to a man named Jeremiah. God said, "When you call upon me and come and pray to me, I will hear you" (Jeremiah 29:12). You can always reach God. With God, you never get a busy signal. God hears you when you pray.

Must we always pray out loud? No. God hears us even when we don't say our thoughts out loud. When we pray, just as when we're talking to another friend, it's important that we don't do all the talking. We need to be quiet and listen so God can talk to us. God wants to teach us, guide us, provide for us, and care for us. God wants to protect us and help us to be all that he created us to be.

God is big enough and powerful enough to run the universe and care for each one of us at the same time. God answers each prayer in order to give you God's best. Sometimes, God's answer is, "Wait." Sometimes, God's answer is, "No." But remember that God's answer is always part of God's bigger plan for us. God loves us more than we can imagine.

When should we pray? Is there one time that is better than any other time to pray? You can pray when you're swimming, playing hide-and-seek, climbing a tree, or standing on your head. You can pray when you get into a car, while you're riding, and when you arrive safely at the place you wanted to go. You can talk to God silently or out loud when you're playing ball, walking backward, building sand castles, or climbing monkey bars. You can talk to God when you wake up, before you sleep, when you're happy, when you're sad, even when you're lonely, tired, or angry. When we go to a restaurant to eat, let's not forget to thank God for our food there, too, just as we do at home. It's a good way to remind other people to be thankful, too.

Jesus invites us to pray often because God hears us whenever we pray, wherever we pray, and however we pray. There is no wrong time or place to talk and listen to God, our best friend.

Let pretzels be a reminder to you and your family that God is always ready to hear us.

OPTIONAL: STRETCHING FURTHER
Encourage children to share prayers they have learned to say at mealtime or bedtime. How do they feel when everyone says the same prayer? Are they interested in learning a new or different prayer to say with their families?

Today let's cross our arms and bow our heads while we pray. Please repeat after me.

Dear God, we are so glad that we can talk to you. Thank you for hearing us. Thank you for loving us. Help us to listen and to learn how you want us to live. We pray in Jesus' name. Amen.

(If appropriate, give pretzels to children.)

12
Are You Sleeping?

THEME: We need to be aware of temptation and pray that we will be strong against it.

SCRIPTURE: Stay awake and pray that you may not come into the time of trial (or temptation); the spirit indeed is willing, but the flesh is weak.—Matthew 26:41.

PREPARATION: Cut a 9" x 12" piece of tagboard or cardboard into two pieces, each measuring 4 1/2" x 12". With a broad marker, print "watch" on one card and "pray" on the other. (Optional: Bring a phonograph record to show children who may never have seen one.)

Today, we're going to talk about a word that can mean several different things. (*Show card with "watch" on it.*) Who knows this word? Who knows what this word means? (*Explore various meanings: wristwatch; to look at; to pay attention; to look out; to be careful of.*) What does a watchman (or watchdog) do? A watchman is a guard or a lookout; he keeps watch over a place. Sometimes, when bad weather is coming, we will see across the bottom of the television screen or hear words like "thunderstorm watch" or "winter storm watch" so that we can get ready and be safe when it comes.

In the story we're going to hear today, listen carefully for still another way the word "watch" is used. In Matthew 26, we read that Jesus went with his disciples to a place called Gethsemane. It was like a garden where olive trees grew. He told his disciples to sit down while he went a little further on to pray. Peter, James, and John were among the first men Jesus had called to follow him, and he took these three men with him. Jesus knew that something very painful was going to happen to him. He was sad and troubled and anxious, and he said to Peter, James, and John, "remain here, and stay awake with me" (Matthew 26:38). Then he went on a little further and began to pray. *(If an artist's depiction of Jesus praying is nearby, perhaps in stained glass, call attention to it.)*

When he went back to his followers, he found them sleeping. He said to Peter, "So, could you not stay awake with me one hour? Stay awake and pray that you may not come into the time of trial (or temptation); the spirit indeed is willing, but the flesh is weak" (Matthew 26:40–41). An earlier translation of the Bible (RSV) says, "Watch with me. . . . Watch and pray that you may not enter into temptation."

Again, Jesus went away and prayed. When he came back to his followers the second time, they were asleep again. So he left them sleeping and went back to praying to his Father, God. The third time he came back to the sleeping disciples, he told them to get up because Judas had come with the men who would arrest Jesus.

What did Jesus mean when he said, "Watch with me"? (*Stay awake.*) When he found them sleeping the second time, he said "Watch and pray." Not only did he want them to stay awake, he wanted them to pray. What should they pray for? They should pray for strength against temptation. Jesus knew there would be times when his followers would *want* to do what they knew was right, but they would do what seemed easier at that time, even if they knew it was wrong. As it happened, when Jesus was arrested, his disciples ran away. Later on, they lied and said they didn't even know him.

Have you ever done something you knew was wrong to do? Maybe Mom had just baked or bought some cookies. Mom might have said, "Don't eat a cookie before dinner. It will spoil your appetite." You knew you should obey your mother, but that cookie looked so good, and you thought you just couldn't wait. So, when Mom wasn't looking, you took one and ate it. Has anything like that ever happened to you?

Sometimes you know in your head or in your heart that there are good reasons that you shouldn't eat or drink something, but your tummy wins the argument. Jesus said, "The spirit is willing, but the flesh is weak." When the disciples fell asleep, they may have wanted to stay awake—to "watch" with Jesus—but their bodies were tired, and their eyelids felt so heavy that they couldn't keep their eyes open.

*I remember something that happened to me when I was a little girl. I was at my friend Betty's house. At that time, we didn't have cassette tapes or CDs, but Betty had some records and a record player. (*Optional: Show record.*) She put a record on, and Betty and her brother Jay and I listened to the songs on the record. We were sitting on the floor and the records were on the floor, too. I moved around a little bit and I felt a kind of crunch or cracking sound under me. I knew I had broken one of her records. I felt so bad that I didn't want to tell Betty. But she soon noticed the broken record, and she went yelling and crying to her Mom, "Jay broke one of my records!" She wanted him to be punished. I didn't say anything. I just went home. I wanted to tell Betty—I knew that I should have—but I guess I was a little afraid to do that. I didn't want Betty to be angry with me. But neither did I want her brother to be punished for something I did.

I told my mother what happened, and then I went back to Betty's house and told her and her mother, and I said I was sorry. I'm not exactly sure, but I think my mother gave money so Betty could get a new record.

We don't know when or how we will be tested or tempted to do something we know is wrong. That's why Jesus said that we should watch and pray for strength to do what is right.

There are two words we need to remember. (*Hold up "watch" card.*) What does this say? The word "watch" means to pay attention, to look out for times and places where we could be tempted to do something wrong. What must we do so we will be strong enough to do the right thing? (*Hold up "pray" card.*) Yes, we must pray, just as Jesus did.

OPTIONAL: STRETCHING FURTHER
Read Matthew 26:36–45 to see what Jesus did to resist temptation. (*Pray to God, seek support of friends and loved ones; focus on the purpose God has given us.*)

Let's pray together now. (*Ask children to bow their heads and repeat after you. Say short, meaningful phrases.*)

Dear God, thank you for your child, Jesus. We are glad that Jesus prayed to you. You made him strong enough to do what you wanted him to do. Help us to look out for temptation. Give us strength to be true to you. In Jesus' name we pray. Amen.

13
The Greatest

THEME: The greatest one is the one who serves.

SCRIPTURE: The greatest among you must become like the youngest, and the leader like one who serves. . . . But I am among you as one who serves.—Luke 22:26–27

PREPARATION: Cut an 8 1/2" x 11" piece of tagboard (poster board) or cardboard into two pieces about 4" x 11". Cut an identical third piece. With a broad, black marker, print each of the following words on a card: "look," "listen," "love."

Does anyone here like football? basketball? baseball? soccer? I noticed that each team wants to be number one. What does that mean? Yes, number one means that team has won the most games. They think they are the best team. Which would you rather be—number eleven or number one? a winner or a loser? the slowest runner in a race or the fastest? When you're waiting in line for lunch, would you rather be last in line or first? On a paper at school, would you rather get the highest mark or the lowest? Would you rather be the president or the one who shines the president's shoes?

We all want to be the best, the most important, the greatest, don't we? *On papers that some of my fifth-grade students gave to me, they liked to sign their names, "Brad the greatest" or "Julie the greatest." They wanted me to think that they could do something, or everything, better than anyone else. It usually wasn't true!

In Luke, we read that Jesus' disciples argued among themselves about which of them was the greatest, the most important. But Jesus said, "The greatest among you must become like the youngest, and the leader like one who serves. . . . I am among you as one who serves"

(Luke 22:26–27). He meant that the most important person should be like the least important person, and the leader should be like a servant.

Then he showed the disciples how to be a servant: [During supper (with them) . . . Jesus] "got up from the table, took off his outer robe, and tied a towel around himself. Then he poured water into a basin and began to wash the disciples' feet and to wipe them with the towel that was tied around him" (John 13:4–5). This was a job that the servants or slaves usually did when a guest came to the house. It was a polite thing to do, and it was necessary. Their shoes were like sandals and their feet were very dirty from walking or traveling on dusty roads.

Then Jesus said, "You call me Teacher and Lord—and you are right, for that is what I am. So if I, your Lord and Teacher, have washed your feet, you also ought to wash one another's feet. For I have set you an example, that you also should do as I have done to you" (John 13:13–15). Jesus was the most important person in the room, and he did a servant's job—the lowest job—for his disciples. He was teaching them to be servants, doing things for one another. He was teaching them, too, that there is no job that they should be too proud to do. We show our love by doing things for one another—whatever it is that needs to be done.

Later, the older leaders, the leading priests and teachers of the law, came together. They asked Jesus, "Are you . . . the Son of God?" He said to them, "You say that I am" (Luke 22:70).

Then they took Jesus to Pilate, the Roman governor of Judea. Pilate asked him, "Are you the king of the Jews?" He answered, "You say so" (Luke 23:1–3). Jesus had done nothing wrong, but the leaders of the Jews wanted him to die because he had said that he was the Christ, the child of God.

When Jesus hung on the cross, a sign above him said, "This is the King of the Jews" (Luke 23:38). At that time people didn't understand what it really meant. Now we know that Jesus *is* the ruler of the Jews—and of everyone else in the whole universe! He is the greatest person who ever lived in this world. He is God's child, and he never disobeyed God, and he never sinned. But he took the punishment for what *we*—you and I—have done wrong. He died, but he rose again. If we believe in him, we can have new life with him, too.

How can you be a servant like Jesus? *(Encourage children to suggest appropriate ways of serving.)* Think of the people you see everyday. What could you do for your mother or father to make their work a little easier? What could you do for a brother or sister? for your grandparents, teacher, bus driver, or baby-sitter? You might help a younger child to wash hands before and after dinner. You can put toys away when you're done playing with them. If someone has a heavy load, offer to help carry some books or packages. When you have a chance to pick people to be on your team for a game, maybe you could choose first the person who is always picked last, or choose the one with the saddest face. Maybe you could rake leaves or shovel snow for a neighbor who can't do it.

Here are three words to help you to remember how to be a servant. *(Hold up "look" card.)* The first word is "look." *(Give children a chance to say the word if they know it.)* "Look" for times and places and people whom you might serve. *(Ask children to say the word "look" together.)* The second word is "listen." *(Hold up "listen" card. Say "listen" together.)* "Listen" to what others say. Don't think only of your own ideas, what you want, and what you want to say. The third word is "love." *(Hold up "love" card. Say "love.")* Show "love" to everyone!

Did you notice something alike in these three words? Yes, they all begin with the letter "L." Let's see if you can say them again. To be a servant, you are going to "look," "listen," and "love!"

OPTIONAL: STRETCHING FURTHER

Suggest appropriate ways that children might be servants for Jesus to needy people and persons with disabilities in their community. Another possibility could be ways that children can contribute to the church's missions in other parts of the country or the world.

Let's Pray: *(Ask children to bow their heads and repeat after you. Say short, meaningful phrases.)*

Dear God, thank you for sending Jesus to us. He showed us how to be a servant. Help us to look for places and people to serve. Help us to listen to what other people say. Help us to love everyone, just as Jesus did. We pray in his name. Amen.

14
The Eraser

THEME: When we are sorry for what we have done wrong and we ask God to forgive us, God erases the record against us. Jesus took *our* punishment when he died on the cross.

SCRIPTURE: God made you alive together with him, when he forgave us all our trespasses, erasing the record that stood against us with its legal demands. He set this aside, nailing it to the cross.—Colossians 2:13–14

PREPARATION: Obtain pencil erasers to give one to each child. Bring a small slate or chalkboard, a piece of chalk, a chalkboard eraser, and a damp sponge. (You might substitute a marker-board and a colored marker and eraser.)

I brought something to write on today. (*Show chalkboard or marker-board.*) You know what this is, don't you? A long time ago, when my parents were your age, boys and girls didn't have tablets of paper to write on in school. Instead, each student had something like this to write on with chalk. It was called a slate, because it was made of a kind of rock called slate. When a big, black, smooth piece of slate was fastened to a wall, it was called a blackboard. Now there are green ones, too, so we just call them chalkboards.

Where have you seen a chalkboard (or a white marker-board)? *I have one in my kitchen. I use it to write down things that I need from the grocery store. Sometimes my husband writes phone numbers on it, too.

Classrooms usually have big chalkboards or marker-boards fastened to the walls. How might a chalkboard be used in a school or Sunday school classroom? In school, teachers sometimes write names of students on the chalkboard. Whose name shall I write? (*Write the name of a volunteer.*) Sometimes, having your name written on the board means that you haven't finished your work on time. Then you have to keep on working until you're finished, even if the rest of the class has gone outside for exercise and play. When you have finished your work, you can erase your name and join your classmates outside. (*Let the child whose name you wrote come and erase it.*)

If someone does something bad at school, what else might happen? Will that person be punished? Suppose, at home, you tease your brother or sister, or you take a toy away, what might happen? If you keep on teasing or doing something bad after you have been told to stop, might you be punished? Might you have to give up something you like to do? Or might you have to take time out, away from the rest of the family for a while? We don't like to be punished, do we?

In the Bible, we read a song written by a man named David. In Psalm 51:1, he writes, "Have mercy on me, O God . . . blot out my transgressions." Again, in verse 9, David says, "Hide your face from my sins, and blot out all my iniquities." Those words—"transgressions" and "iniquities"—both mean bad, wrong things that are done against God's law. For example, one of God's laws says "You shall not steal" (Exodus 20:15). If you take something that doesn't belong to you, you have broken God's law about stealing. We could say stealing is a transgression, or stealing is an iniquity. An easier word to remember is "sin." Stealing is a sin. David had broken God's laws, but he wanted God to be kind to him and rub or wipe off all the wrong things—the sins—that he had done. David did not want to be punished.

In another part of the Bible, we read a letter that the apostle Paul wrote to people in a place called Colossae. Paul used another word that means sin—"trespasses." He wrote that God "forgave us all our trespasses, *erasing* the record that stood against us . . . He set this aside, nailing it to the cross" (Colossians 2:13–14). Paul says when we are sorry for our sins—the wrong things we have done—and we ask God to forgive us, God *erases* the record against us.

I notice that, even though I erase someone's name from the chalkboard, it still looks a little cloudy, not quite clean. Do you think it might look cleaner if I wipe it with this wet sponge? Let's see. (*Demonstrate.*) This is like what God does when God forgives us. God wipes away the bad things and makes us clean and new. The reason God can wipe our record clean is that Jesus took the punishment for *our* sins when he died on the cross. Jesus was not guilty. He had done nothing wrong in his whole life. He had never sinned, but he gave up his life so we can be forgiven. That's how much God loves us!

I'm going to give each of you a pencil eraser. When you write or draw and you make a mistake, you can use the eraser to rub off the mistake. Let this eraser remind you that all of us sometimes do bad or wrong things. If we are sorry for what we have done, and we ask God to forgive us, God will forgive. God will wipe the slate clean. God will erase the record of what we've done, and God won't even remember it anymore.

We need to keep asking God to forgive us every day. Because none of us is perfect, we make mistakes. We sin. Sometimes we tease, we get angry, we argue, we say unkind things that hurt people. Then we can say we're sorry, and we hope we won't do it again, but we do. So we need to pray and ask God to forgive us every day. A good time to do that is at bedtime. Tonight, think about what happened during the day. Thank God for the good things, and ask God to forgive you for the bad things you did. Sometimes there is something good and kind that we should have done, but we didn't do it. Ask God for help to do better tomorrow.

OPTIONAL: STRETCHING FURTHER
Talk about further steps to take after being sorry for your sins and asking for forgiveness: doing God's will; obeying Jesus' teachings; giving God control of your life; helping others know about God's love; and so on.

Let's pray. (*Ask children to bow their heads and repeat after you. Say short, meaningful phrases.*)

Thank you, God, for loving us. Thank you for sending Jesus to love us, too. We are sorry for doing things that make you sad. Forgive us. Thank you for erasing the record of the things we have done wrong. Thank you for erasing the record of the things that you want us to do, but we didn't do them. We pray in Jesus' name. Amen.

15
Messages

THEME: We are messengers, spreading the good news that Jesus is alive!

SCRIPTURE: Then go quickly and tell his disciples, "He has been raised from the dead."—Matthew 28:7

PREPARATION: Make a child-size banner or signs on sturdy paper, proclaiming "Jesus is alive!" and, "Because I live, you also will live!" (John 14:19). Select an appropriate spot outside the church to post the signs.

---

*Do you know how it happened that I am here with you today? I have a phone answering machine at home. Do some of you have a phone answering machine at home, too? When I came home from the grocery store the other day, my phone machine was beeping and blinking a red light at me. I knew there was a message because the machine's voice said, "You . . . have . . . one . . . message." So I pushed the button to hear the message that someone had left for me. Then I heard Pastor Cindy's voice saying, "Virginia, will you do the Children's Message on Sunday in the 10:45 service?"

I am here to talk with you because I heard Pastor Cindy's message on the phone machine. How else, besides the telephone, can we send and receive messages? (*Encourage responses or suggest talking person-to-person, writing, e-mail, signing.*)

Even what we do with our bodies sends messages. What does it mean if I raise my thumb? (*Demonstrate thumbs-up.*) Yes, thumbs-up means we think something is good, or someone is going to do something well. What message do we send when we do high fives? (*Raise open right hand and slap another open right hand.*) Yes, that means we're celebrating; something has made us happy.

Can you think of times when you have received a written message? Have you ever found a note from Mom or Dad in your shirt or jeans pocket? In your lunch bag or box? Sometimes boys and girls pass messages—notes—to one another when they should be working on something else in school. Have you ever seen that happen? Sometimes a teacher gives you a message to give to your parents. That could be good news or not-so-good news.

Can you think of a special time when you got good news—exciting news? Today, we're going to talk about good news—a message from an angel to two women named Mary and Mary Magdalene. From the book of Matthew, we know that Jesus died on the cross and that his body was laid in a tomb, like a cave in a hillside, with a huge stone rolled in front of the opening. Listen to hear the message from the angel. (*Read aloud Matthew 28:1–8.*)

Did you hear the message? There really are four parts to the angel's message. The first part of the message was: "Don't be afraid. Be happy." The second part was: "Jesus isn't here. He isn't dead. Don't look for him in a grave or a tomb." The third part was: "Come and see. See for yourself that it's true." And fourth: "Go quickly and tell his disciples. Be messengers. Spread the good news."

The message that Jesus lives is indeed good news! Wonderful news! Exciting news! Can you imagine how you would feel if your very best friend had died? You would be very sad to have lost your friend. Then imagine getting a message that says your friend isn't dead! Your friend is alive, and you will see your friend again!

It's especially good news that Jesus is alive, for Jesus said, "Because I live, you also will live" (John 14:19). That means that, if we believe in Jesus, we will die, but we will live again, too. Jesus died and proved that he could live again. Jesus rose from the dead, just as he said he would. We know he keeps his promises.

How do you feel when you get good news? Good news makes me feel happy. When I have good news, I don't want to keep it to myself. I want to tell everyone who will listen. Notice that the angel told Mary and Mary Magdalene, "Go quickly and tell his disciples, 'He has been raised from the dead.' . . . So they left the tomb . . . and ran to tell his disciples" (Matthew 28:7–8). Jesus' friends were so excited that they did go quickly—the Bible says they ran to tell his followers what had happened.

OPTIONAL: STRETCHING FURTHER
Talk about how the Holy Bible is a message from God.

We are to spread the joy, too, and spread the good news that Jesus lives by the power of God. Let's pray first, and then we'll share the good news. (*Ask children to bow their heads and repeat after you.*)

Dear God, we thank you that Jesus is alive. Help us to spread the good news to those who have not heard it. Help us to live as you want us to live every day. We pray in Jesus' name. Amen.

Do you think everyone here this morning already knows the good news we've been talking about? We hope they do! But just in case there is one person who hasn't heard, let's be sure. We are going to shout, "Good news!" Ready? "Good news!"

Congregation, shout back to us. "Good news!"

This time let's shout "Jesus is alive!" (*Repeat as above. If the congregation doesn't respond enthusiastically, try again.*)

I have some signs (or a banner) that tell this exciting, good news, too. Who can read this sign? Yes, it says "Jesus is alive!" Who can read this sign? "Because I live, you also will live" (John 14:19). Who wants to carry a sign? (*Distribute signs.*)

Do you remember what the angel told the women at the tomb? The angel said they should "go quickly and tell" the good news. That's what we are going to do. Let's all stand. If you don't have a sign to carry, you can do thumbs-up or high five. Let's see thumbs-up . . . high five. Let's do thumbs-up or high five with the people we pass. Ready? Follow me. (*Shouting "Good news!" and "Jesus is alive!" go quickly to the exit of the sanctuary. Lead the children, or have a designated adult lead them, outside where they can post the signs for all to see.*)

16
Seeing and Believing

THEME: Though we haven't seen, we believe that Jesus died and God brought him to life again.

SCRIPTURE: Jesus said to him, "Have you believed because you have seen me? Blessed are those who have not seen and yet have come to believe."—John 20:29

PREPARATION: On a piece of cardboard or tagboard about 4" x 8", print "witness" with a dark marker. Gather several Bibles for use in the closing prayer.

Today, we are going to talk about this word—"witness." (*Show card with "witness."*) Do you know what this word—"witness"—means? Let me tell you a story about something you can witness in Florida.

In Florida's warm weather, you can see animals that don't live in colder places. The anhinga is a big, grayish-black bird with a long tail and a long neck. From its head to its tail, it's 28 inches—about this big. (*Demonstrate.*) When the anhinga swims with only its head and long, dark neck out of the water, it looks like a snake. It catches fish to eat, but it doesn't have oil on its feathers like ducks have. So, if it stayed in the water very long, its feathers would be so water-soaked that the bird couldn't swim. It would sink to the bottom.

Walking along a nature trail, you might see an anhinga sitting on a low tree branch hanging over the water. Its big wings, 47 inches wide, (*demonstrate*) are spread out to dry in the sunshine. All of a sudden, the bird dives down into the water, spears a fish with its long, pointed beak, and then comes up and sits on the branch again.

It jerks its head backward several times with the fish still on its beak. The anhinga jerks once more; this time the fish flies up into the air. The bird opens its bill, catches the fish headfirst, and swallows it whole. If you see this happen (*as I did); you are a witness. Sometimes we use the word "eyewitness." You see with your eyes; you are an eyewitness to what the anhinga did.

Do you think we can learn more about being a witness from the Holy Bible? Let's think about Easter. Who knows why we celebrate Easter? Did something special happen? Yes, we celebrate—we're very happy—because God brought Jesus to life again after Jesus had died. Let's listen to the Word of God. I am going to read from the book written by the apostle John. John was an eyewitness to Jesus' empty tomb. (Read John 20:11–18.)

Did anyone see God raising Jesus from the dead—from his grave? No, but when Mary Magdalene and Mary went to the tomb on the third day after Jesus died, they were the first ones to see that the tomb was empty. Then Jesus showed himself to Mary Magdalene and talked to her outside the tomb. Mary Magdalene was an eyewitness. She saw and spoke with Jesus after he rose from the dead.

Let's hear verse 19. (Read John 20:19.) That evening, Jesus came and stood among the disciples and talked with them. The disciples, too, were witnesses that Jesus was alive.

Listen again. (Read verse 20.) Why did Jesus show the disciples his hands and side? (Jesus had been nailed to the cross where he died. The nails left holes in his hands or wrists. To make sure that he was dead, a soldier had pierced Jesus' side with a sword.) Now, the disciples were happy. Here was Jesus, and he was alive!

Listen while I read verses 24–28. (Read aloud.) Was Thomas happy when the other disciples told him they had seen Jesus? No, Thomas doubted that the other disciples had seen Jesus alive. He wouldn't believe it. Not even ten friends could change Thomas's mind. He had to see for himself. He had to be an eyewitness. Through many years, we have come to use the word "doubt" when we talk about Thomas, the disciple. Sometimes when someone is unsure, full of doubt about something, we call that person a "doubting Thomas," even if the person's name is not Thomas.

Jesus was kind to Thomas. He showed Thomas the nail marks in his hands and the wound in his side so that Thomas would believe it was really Jesus, alive. Does that mean that we can believe only what we see? No, we believe in many things we can't see. Can we see the wind? No, but we can see leaves being blown, branches moving, and kites flying because of the wind. What other things do we believe in, even though we can't see them? (*Kindness, courage, love, joy, friendship; an electric current moving through an electric cord; microwaves cooking food; radio and television signals.*) When you flip the switch on the wall or on an electric lamp, you know the light will go on, unless the bulb is burned out.

Believing beyond what we can see is called having faith. Having faith means being sure, even when you can't see proof, even when you are not an eyewitness. Jesus said to Thomas, "Blessed are those who have not seen and yet have come to believe" (John 20:29). That's why we are so happy at Easter time. We believe in Jesus and we are blessed. He was dead. Now he's alive. Because he lives, we, too, will live. We will live forever with him!

OPTIONAL: STRETCHING FURTHER

Are there people today who don't believe in Jesus? Yes, we are sad to say that many people do not know about Jesus, or they have heard, but don't believe that Jesus is the child of God.

Some people think they would believe in Jesus if they could see a sign or a miracle. But we have all the proof we need in the words of the Bible and in the words of people who are witnesses to what God has done. The apostle John tells us that that is why he wrote this book. (*Read aloud John 20:30–31.*)

Have you ever seen in court or on television someone raising one hand while resting the other hand on the Bible? This usually happens when a person is making a very serious promise. At a trial where someone is accused of breaking a law, it could be a promise to tell "the truth, the whole truth, and nothing but the truth" about what you have witnessed. Putting your hand on the Bible means that you are calling on God to be a witness that what you say is true. If you are beginning a very important job, like being the president of a country, putting your hand on the Bible can mean, too, that you are calling on God to be a witness that you will do what you have promised to do.

Before we pray today, I'd like all of you to gather in closely so everyone can touch the Bible I'm holding. (*If the group is very large, use several Bibles in several small groups.*) Putting our hands on the Bible helps us to know that we are talking to God when we pray. We are all members of God's family. God's Word is for everyone.

Let's pray. (*Ask children to bow their heads and repeat after you. Say short, meaningful phrases.*)

Dear God, we believe in Jesus. We believe in your Word. We believe in you. Even though we can't see you, we feel you in our hearts. Thank you for your love that lasts forever. We pray in the name of Jesus, our Savior. Amen.

17
Treasures

THEME: Storing up treasures in heaven is far more important than collecting treasures on earth.

SCRIPTURE: Where your treasure is, there your heart will be also.—Matthew 6:21; Luke 12:34

PREPARATION: Gather a collection of one kind of things, either stuffed animals or trading cards, seashells, coins, stamps, arrowheads, soda can tabs, and so forth. Put them in a box—a "treasure chest." Use a Bible that will fit into the box.

I brought a treasure chest to show you today. Do you believe that this is a treasure chest? What is treasure? Treasure is something that is valuable. It's stored away. It could be worth a lot of money.

Can you guess what treasure I have stored in this box? Would you like to see? (*Show one item from the collection.*) *A friend of mine carved this bird from wood. Do you know what kind of bird it is? It's an owl. Why do you think this owl is a treasure? It's a treasure because my friend carved it by hand with a knife. He spent many hours shaping it, carving out individual feathers, and painting it. There is no other owl that looks exactly like this one. I like owls. I think they look like smart birds; we even call them wise owls. I treasure this one.

Do you think it's all right for me to think of this owl, made of wood, as a treasure? What if I bowed down to this owl and prayed to it and sang hymns to it? Would that be all right, too? No, if I worshiped this owl, I would be treating this wooden bird the way I should be treating only God. God created all the animals, including owls, and I can admire what God created, and I can admire my friend's creation—the wooden owl.

But worshiping this wooden owl that looks like something God created would be wrong. It would be a sin.

Let's see what else is inside my treasure box. *(Bring out the remaining items.)* Well, look at that! More owls! What do you notice about these owls? Are they all the same, or different? *(Call attention to different sizes, shapes, colors, poses, and materials.)* Is it all right for me to think of all of these owls as treasures? *(Encourage various responses.)*

Listen to what Jesus says about treasure: "Where your treasure is, there your heart will be also" (Matthew 6:21; Luke 12:34). *(Repeat verse.)* I think that means that we will spend the most time and energy and money on whatever is most important to us. If I spend so much time and energy and money on shopping and buying owls for my collection that I'm not giving my time and energy and money to do things for the church, my family, and my neighbors, it's not okay. If I become so proud of my owl collection that it's more important to me than anything else, I have let my owl collection become my God, and that's a sin.

I've been talking about my collection and me. Do any of you like to collect things? *(Encourage children to tell what they collect: stuffed animals, seashells, coins, stamps, rocks, trading cards, arrowheads, awards, soda can tabs.)* It's fun to collect things, isn't it?

I know that you are not going to worship your collections. That would be silly. But do you ever get so busy with your collection or your toys that you forget to help Mom or Dad? Do you ever get so interested in playing, or collecting, or watching television that you don't do your homework or what Mom and Dad have asked you to do? Have you ever been thinking so much about your treasures that you don't hear what your teacher is saying? Have you ever looked at someone else's toys or collection and thought, "I wish they were mine"? What if you wanted what someone else has so much that you took it? You would be letting those *things* you treasure become too important to you. You would be breaking God's laws.

Let's hear more about what Jesus says about treasures. *(Read aloud Matthew 6:19–20.)*

What can happen to my collection of owls? *(They can be broken, lost, stolen, burned.)* Jesus says that things made from metal, like bicycles and toy cars, can get rusty. Things made from cloth, like stuffed animals, can be destroyed by moths. These kinds of treasures won't last forever.

So Jesus says that we should store up for ourselves treasures in heaven, where they can't be destroyed. How can we do that? We can store treasures in heaven by doing what God wants us to do. God wants us to believe that Jesus is God's child. God wants us to love and care for one another and forgive those who do wrong to us.

Those kinds of treasures—love, faith, and forgiveness—can't be bought with money. They can't be lost or broken or stolen or burned. Our most valuable treasure of all is Jesus. He loves us and lives in us, and we have his words and promises in the Holy Bible. I'm going to put this Bible in my treasure chest to remind me that loving and serving God and caring for others is much more important than the *things* I have. Maybe you would like to put a Bible in or near your "treasure" at home, too. Another good place to put your Bible is near your bed, so that you can remind whoever puts you to bed at night to read to you from the Bible every day. We treasure the Bible, too, because it is full of God's love. The Bible itself is like a treasure chest. Remember, "Where your treasure is, there your heart will be also."

OPTIONAL: STRETCHING FURTHER
Read aloud 2 Timothy 3:15–17. Talk about the Bible—scripture inspired by God—as a treasure chest of wisdom that teaches us how to live. The Bible tells us that God loves us; how to show our love for God (*by being obedient*); and how to love other people (*being kind, forgiving, merciful.*)

Let's pray. (*Ask children to bow their heads and repeat after you. Say short, meaningful phrases.*)

Dear God, we thank you for treasures in heaven. We thank you for love. We thank you for Jesus, the best treasure of all. Help us to know what is most important in our lives. We pray in Jesus' name. Amen.

18

A Word with God

THEME: God talks to us through the Bible—God's Word.

SCRIPTURE: All scripture is inspired by God and is useful for teaching, for reproof, for correction, and for training in righteousness, so that everyone who belongs to God may be proficient, equipped for every good work.—2 Timothy 3:16–17

PREPARATION: Bring an old lantern or oil lamp and a flashlight. Print or type "Your word is a lamp to my feet and a light to my path—Psalm 119:105" on paper or tagboard strips to be copied and cut apart as bookmarks, about 2 1/2" x 8 1/2". (An alternative might be to purchase commercially made bookmarks or stickers stating this scripture.) Find out what your church is doing to provide Bibles to those who have none. How can the children help?

Have you ever been sitting somewhere, maybe with other children, watching a show or a program, when someone came and tapped you on the shoulder and said, "I need to talk to you"? Maybe you've been on the playground and a grownup said, "I want a word with you." Maybe someone has beckoned you to come. (*Demonstrate.*) What did you do? Did you want to know what the person was going to say to you? What news or word was so important that you couldn't finish what you were doing?

We use words to say many things. Some words make us feel good and happy. Can you think of some happy words? (*Vacation, ice cream, Christmas, the beach.*) Some words make us feel bad or sad. (*Broken, goodbye, hurts, sick.*) But the most important word of all is the Word of God. Where can we find the Word of God? The Bible is called the Word of God, and God's Word is good.

Did God do the actual writing of this book? The Bible was actually written by more than forty people, including fishermen, doctors, kings, priests, shepherds, a tax collector, a soldier, and a butler. The writers lived on three continents—three different parts of the world. How long do you think it took these people to write the Bible? It took more than 1,500 years!

Then why do we call the Bible the Word of God? We call it the Word of God because God inspired the writers. God gave them the thoughts to write down. Let's hear what the apostle Paul wrote in a letter to a man named Timothy. (Read aloud 2 Timothy 3:16–17.) The Bible is the inspired Word of God, helping us to know how God wants us to live.

Reading or hearing the Bible is like getting a letter from God to us. And sometimes it feels like God is tapping us on the shoulder, calling us aside, saying "I want to have a word with you. Remember to be kind. Remember to share. Remember to forgive. Remember what Jesus did."

Have you ever received something that had to be put together before you could use it? (A kite; model airplane, boat or car; action figure; bookcase.) Usually, in the package, there's a piece of paper with drawings to show you how to put it together. If you don't follow the directions carefully, it doesn't fit together right. You might even have some pieces left over. You might end up with a bookcase instead of a bed! The Bible is like a book of directions; it tells us what to do so that all the pieces of our lives fit together so we can do good work for God.

When we read or hear the Bible, we notice that some parts of it are short; other parts are long. Do you know which is the longest chapter in the Bible? It's near the middle of the Bible—Psalm 119. It has 176 verses and 22 sections. Each section begins with a different letter of the Hebrew alphabet. That made it easier for people to memorize it. People didn't have their own copies of the Hebrew Bible long ago, so they memorized scripture and passed it on by repeating it.

Can you guess what this very long psalm is about? Psalm 119 is all about God's Word, which we have in the Bible. Verse 105 says, "Your word is a lamp to my feet and a light to my path." Have you ever been in a place at night when the electricity went off, maybe because there was a storm? Have you ever been outside at night, maybe in the woods or a park, without any light? It can be a little scary if you can't see where you are or where you are stepping. Long ago, people used a lamp or a lantern (*show*) to light their way. A flashlight (*show*) makes me feel safer in the darkness. The Bible can show us the way to live so we will stay on the path that God wants us to choose.

In the Bible we read: "The grass withers, the flower fades; but the word of our God will stand forever" (Isaiah 40:8; see also 1 Peter 1:24b–25). Do you know that the Bible has been read by more people, in more languages, than any other book? Millions of Bibles and parts of Bibles are sold or given out every year around the world, in hundreds of languages. The Bible and the truth it teaches will never be destroyed. It will never go out of style. No other book can take its place. We can always count on the Word of God. "The Lord exists forever; your word is firmly fixed in heaven," we read in Psalm 119:89.

What is the world's all-time bestseller, the greatest book, the best book ever? The Bible shows us how to live and promises that we shall go on living! I'm not going to ask you to memorize the 176 verses of Psalm 119, but I would like you to remember one verse— number 105: "Your word is a lamp to my feet and a light to my path." (*Hand out bookmarks. If time permits, let the children repeat after you as you recite the verse in short phrases.*) Maybe your parents will help you so that next Sunday we can all say it together.

OPTIONAL: STRETCHING FURTHER

Talk about Psalm 119:105. How can the Bible show us the way ahead so we won't stumble or fall? (*As we learn God's Words and obey God's laws and commandments, we become loving people who help others and live for God.*)

Let's pray. (*Ask children to bow their heads and repeat after you. Say short, meaningful phrases.*)

Dear God, we thank you for your Word. Help us to understand what you want us to learn. Thank you for loving us. Help us to love you more and more each day. We pray in Jesus' name. Amen.

19
In Tune with Jesus

THEME: Being in tune with Jesus means that whatever we do and say brings honor to his name.

SCRIPTURE: As God's chosen ones, holy and beloved, clothe yourselves with compassion, kindness, humility, meekness, and patience. Bear with one another and, if anyone has a complaint against another, forgive each other; just as the Lord has forgiven you, so you also must forgive. Above all, clothe yourselves with love, which binds everything together in perfect harmony. And let the peace of Christ rule in your hearts, to which indeed you were called in the one body. And be thankful. Let the word of Christ dwell in you richly; teach and admonish one another in all wisdom; and with gratitude in your hearts sing psalms, hymns, and spiritual songs to God. And whatever you do, in word or deed, do everything in the name of the Lord Jesus, giving thanks to God the Father through him.—Colossians 3:12–17

PREPARATION: Arrange for vocalists or instrumentalists to demonstrate playing or singing out of tune, and then in tune with one another. (Optional: Bring at least nine assorted items of children's clothes in a laundry basket.)

(*Comment on the beauty of the elements of music heard so far in worship today.*) I really liked hearing the choir (or soloist) sing (or pianist, organist, instrumentalists play) today. It felt like "a joyful noise to the Lord." Did you like it, too? (*If appropriate, say, "Let's all clap for them" or, "Let's all say thank you to them."*)

In order to sing (or play) so beautifully, they had to do a lot of practicing together. Do you know what the choir does before they even start to practice singing? (*As prearranged, ask vocalists or instrumentalists to demonstrate being out of tune with one another, piano, or organ.*) Oh! That sounds awful, doesn't it? There must be something else to do! (*As prearranged, musicians demonstrate getting in tune with one another.*) Oh! Doesn't that sound much better when everyone is in tune? Thank you, musicians.

You know that the early Christians had only the Hebrew Scriptures for their Bible. The rest of the Bible hadn't been written yet. So they memorized what they knew about Jesus and passed on, from person to person, their stories about him. Sometimes they passed on the stories and the lessons by singing them. So music became an important part of worship (and Sunday school). It's important for people who sing or play instruments together to be in tune. If they were out of tune, no one would want to listen to them.

It's even more important that all of us be in tune with Jesus. How can we do that? In the Christian Scripture part of the Bible, we read a letter that the apostle Paul wrote (while in prison in Rome) to the believers in Jesus Christ in a city called Colossae. (*Read Colossians 3:12–17 from a Bible.*) Paul wrote that Christians should sing to God. And he wrote that God wants us to be like Jesus in everything we do and say.

How will we act if we live like Jesus? (*Encourage responses from children. Reread portions of scripture aloud, pausing to ask children if they know the meaning of these words: compassion—feeling sad for someone who's hurting, and wanting to help; kindness; humility—not acting proud or more important than others; meekness—being gentle; patience—waiting without complaining; forgiving—excusing and no longer feeling angry at someone; thankful.*)

We can be in tune with Jesus if we act like he did. And we can show that we love Jesus by loving other people. Paul wrote, "And let the peace of Christ rule in your hearts" (Colossians 3:15). That means if we have an argument or don't agree with someone, we should let the peace that comes from Jesus be the umpire or the referee in our hearts. Settle the argument by choosing the way that will give us that good feeling of peace.

Another way to get in tune and stay in tune with Jesus is by praying. Jesus is our leader and we need to stay connected to him.

This week, when you sing or hear music, let it remind you that you need to be in tune with Jesus. And when you pray, ask God to help you to be kind and loving like Jesus.

OPTIONAL: STRETCHING FURTHER

"As God's chosen ones, holy and beloved, clothe yourselves with compassion, kindness, humility, meekness, and patience. Bear with one another and, if anyone has a complaint against another, forgive each other. . . . Above all, clothe yourselves with love. . . . And let the peace of Christ rule in your hearts. . . . And be thankful" (Colossians 3:12–15). Here, Paul compares the way we should act to putting on clothes. (*Hand out articles of clothes for children to put on, saying, "Who wants to put on forgiveness? thankfulness?)* Each day, as you get dressed, remember to put on the things that will help you to be in tune with Jesus, too.

Let's pray. (*Ask children to bow their heads and repeat after you. Say short, meaningful phrases.*)

Dear God, thank you for the apostle Paul and the letters that he wrote. Thank you for the gift of music. Help us to be kind and loving and forgiving. We want to be like Jesus and in tune with him. Amen.

20
A Time for Growing

THEME: God, the Creator, is the One who makes things grow.

SCRIPTURE: What then is Apollos? What is Paul? Servants through whom you came to believe, as the Lord assigned to each. I planted, Apollos watered, but God gave the growth. So neither the one who plants nor the one who waters is anything, but only God who gives the growth. The one who plants and the one who waters have a common purpose, and each will receive wages according to the labor of each. For we are God's servants, working together; you are God's field, God's building.—1 Corinthians 3:5–9

PREPARATION: 1.) Bring several vegetable or flower seeds of various sizes, such as carrot, celery, corn, bean, and an onion or flower bulb. Bring seed packets or pictures of the "fruit" of these seeds and bulbs; 2.) Make enough copies of the Honey Carrots recipe (see page 68) to give one to each child. Tape or glue one carrot seed to the top of the recipe.

(*Show several tiny seeds to children.*) Can you see what is in my hand? Yes, they are seeds. If I plant these seeds, what do you think will happen? What will grow? We don't know what will grow without looking at the picture on the packet. (*Show picture or packet.*) But God knows, because God made everything that grows. And God created each tiny seed so that it will grow and make another fruit or flower or vegetable just like the plant it came from. Isn't that amazing?

(Show the larger seeds and bulbs, one at a time.) Do you know what will grow if I plant this seed? If I want tomatoes to grow in my garden, could I plant this (corn or bean) and expect a tomato plant to grow? Why not? Wouldn't it be a good joke on me if I put this kernel of corn in the ground and up came spinach?

What is your favorite vegetable? Carrots are one of my favorites. *(Show carrot seed.)* God made each tiny seed to sprout stems and leaves and a root that will become another carrot. If I wanted to have carrots grow in my garden, what would I need to do? *(Plant the right seeds, in good soil, in a sunny spot.)* Can I just forget about the seeds and wait for them to grow more carrots? No. I need to be sure that the seeds and the plants that grow from them have enough water. I need to pull weeds that might grow near the carrot plants. But if God didn't create the seeds, and provide the soil, the rain, the sunshine, and the right temperatures, the seeds we plant couldn't grow.

Now think about this with me. Are you amazed when you see what people's inventions can do? A telephone lets us hear voices and talk to people who are far, far away. A television set lets us watch and hear programs around the world. A computer lets us send and receive information from almost anywhere in the world. It lets us hear sounds, and type and correct, and it remembers what we've written. Rockets blast off and send people into space, to the moon, or to another planet. A little disk of plastic, called a CD or a DVD, lets us get information or play music or see a movie. These are things that people have invented that seem almost like magic to me. But nothing that people have discovered or made is as wonderful and amazing as the seeds that God made.

In the Bible, we read letters from a man named Paul to the people of the church in a city called Corinth. Paul wrote, "I planted, Apollos watered." He meant that he told them the story of Jesus' life on Earth. His teaching about Jesus was like planting the seed of an idea in their hearts and minds. Apollos was a teacher, too. He helped the believers in Jesus to learn more and more about Jesus and to grow stronger in their faith. Paul wrote, "but God gave the growth." God is the one who made the seed grow as they learned more about Jesus and the way Jesus wants them to live.

Paul goes on to say, "The one who plants and the one who waters have a common purpose, and each will receive wages according to the labor of each." There are people who help to plant and water the seeds of truth and faith in our lives. Our parents, our pastors, teachers, and other believers in Jesus can help us to grow in our understanding about God and Jesus and to keep on growing as long as we live. Paul wrote, "For we are God's servants, working together. . . ."

And he wrote, "You are God's field, God's building." Each of us, too, has been made by God to do some kind of work for him. We, ourselves, are growing like plants in a garden as we learn more about God and the work he wants us to do. Only God knows what we will become.

I'm going to give each of you a recipe. I call it "Honey Carrots." It is a favorite dish that I like to cook and serve to guests. Some of my guests have told me they never liked carrots until they ate them cooked like this. Maybe you could help whoever is cooking at your house to make "Honey Carrots," too. The little carrot seed pasted on the recipe is a reminder that God does amazing things. God is the One who makes things grow, even you and me.

HONEY CARROTS

4 medium carrots, sliced

2 tbs. butter or margarine

1 tbs. honey

3 tbs. water

1/4 tsp. salt

Combine all ingredients in a one-quart glass casserole. Cover with glass lid or plastic wrap. Microwave on HIGH for five minutes. Stir and continue cooking for three to four minutes or until carrots are tender-crisp. Let stand, covered, three minutes before serving. 2 to 3 servings.

OPTIONAL: STRETCHING FURTHER

Find Genesis 1—the first chapter in the first book in the Bible. Read verses 11 to 13 and verses 29 to 31. Talk about God's work on the third day—creating plants for food.

Let's pray. (*Ask children to bow their heads and repeat after you. Say short, meaningful phrases.*)

Dear God, thank you for all the things that you made to grow. Thank you for making me grow, too. Help me to find and do the work that you want me to do. Help me to be what you want me to be. We pray in Jesus' name. Amen.

21
Playing Hide-and-Seek with God

THEME: We can find God in the Bible. We can't hide from God.

SCRIPTURE: When you search for me, you will find me; if you seek me with all your heart, I will let you find me, says the Lord.—Jeremiah 29:13–14

PREPARATION: Cut string into 4" pieces so that each child will receive one. "Hide" one piece in plain sight in the area where you will meet and teach the children.

Let's talk about a game today. Do you like to play hide-and-seek? Do you play it inside or outside? If I didn't know how to play hide-and-seek, how would you explain it to me? So, everyone runs and hides except one person. That person covers her or his eyes and counts. How far does the person count? Does the counter let everyone know when she or he is finished counting? The counter might call out, "Coming!" or, "Here I come, ready or not!" Then the counter becomes the seeker, trying to find the hiders. What happens next? (*Ask children to tell what the seeker does when she or he sees a hider. What does the hider do? Procedures differ. Variations include the seeker calling out the name of the hider and the place where she or he has been seen, such as, "Lisa! Behind the tree!" The two players race for "home" — the place where the seeker did the counting. The game continues until all hiders have run home. The first of the hiders to lose the race is the seeker next time.*)

We don't know who "invented" the game of hide-and-seek. We don't know exactly when children started to play this game, but we know that some of the rules of the game were made thousands of years ago, long before Jesus was born. Jesus might have played hide-and-seek with his friends when he was a boy.

Boys and girls everywhere play hide-and-seek, but they call it different names. Long ago in Scotland, it was called "Hospy." In the country of Greece, it is called "Kreefto." You might hear it called "I Spy" or "Hide-and-Go-Seek."

Children call out different words, too, during the game. The counter might show that she or he has finished counting by calling out, "All hid"; "Whoop"; "Bushel of wheat! Bushel of Rye! All that aren't ready call out 'I'"; or "One! Two! Three! Look out for me!"

When you play hide-and-seek, would you rather be a hider or a seeker? With whom do you play the game?

Could you play hide-and-seek with God? Can you hide from God? Let's see what the Bible says. In a letter to the people called Hebrews, we read, "Before him no creature is hidden" (Hebrews 4:13). That means that nothing and no one in the entire world can be hidden from God. We can't hide from God. God sees us wherever we are: at home, under the bed, behind the door, in the bushes, in school, at church, in a store, in a car, on a boat, in an airplane, or on the playground. God sees us when we are happy, and when we are sad, awake and asleep, good and bad. God sees us all the time: in daytime and nighttime; in spring, summer, fall, and winter; when it's sunny and when it's dark and cloudy.

We can't hide from God, but God can hide *us*—from danger and from things that could hurt us. God hides us like a mother bird protects her young by covering them with her wings (Psalm 17:8).

Suppose you wanted to find God, where would you look? It would be a different kind of seeking, because God doesn't have a body exactly like ours. God is invisible to us. In *our* bodies, we can be in only one place at a time, but God can be everywhere all the time. *(Repeat.)* God can be everywhere all the time.

A long time ago, God told a man named Jeremiah, "When you search for me, you will find me; if you seek me with all your heart, I will let you find me" (Jeremiah 29:13–14).

So where would you begin to look to find God? The Bible helps us to find God. In it we read that Jesus said, "Whoever has seen me has seen the Father" (John 14:9). Jesus is the image of the invisible God. He shows us what God is like. Jesus is God in a human body. Jesus is God. The more we learn about Jesus, the more we are learning about God. And the more we are learning about God, the more we are *finding* God.

Look at this piece of string. I have "hidden" another piece of string just like it. It's hidden near where we are sitting right now. If you see the string I've hidden, don't say anything and don't point to it. Just put your finger up to your lips as if you were going to say, "Sh-h-h." That wasn't hard to find, was it?

When you have played hide-and-seek, has there ever been a person who couldn't be found? The seeker might even give up trying to find a person who has a good hiding place. But God never gives up on you. God loves and protects you. God wants you to find God. Just as God told Jeremiah long ago, "If you seek me with all your heart, I will let you find me." If you try very hard, with your whole self, you will find me.

I'm going to give each of you a piece of string to take with you. You can use it to play "Hide-in-Sight" at home or maybe in school. A fun way to play the game goes like this: Everyone except the hider closes their eyes while the hider hides the string in plain sight, just as I hid the string that you found. Then the seekers get up and walk around, looking for the string. When a seeker finds the string, he or she sits down without saying anything. When everyone is seated, the one who first discovered the string becomes the next hider. Let the string remind you, too, that if you look for God with all your heart, God says, "I will let you find me."

OPTIONAL: STRETCHING FURTHER

Talk about how it feels to know that you can't run and hide from God. When do you feel glad? When do you feel bad? Remind the children that even if we've done something wrong, God still loves us. *If we are sorry and ask God to forgive us, God will forgive.*

Another way to find God is to pray. We can talk to God about *anything* because God already knows everything.

Let's pray. (*Ask children to bow their heads and repeat after you. Say short, meaningful phrases.*)

Dear God, thank you for watching over us. Thank you for never giving up on us. Help us to find you, and help us to be more like Jesus. In his name we pray. Amen.

22
Crystal Clear

THEME: Our task is to let people see God through us.

SCRIPTURE: For it is the God who said, "Let light shine out of darkness," who has shone in our hearts to give the light of the knowledge of the glory of God in the face of Jesus Christ.
—2 Corinthians 4:6

PREPARATION: Obtain a small prism or crystal and a flashlight.

I have something to show you today. (*Show crystal or prism.*) This is called a crystal. What do you notice about it? (*It has many sides. It lets light shine through it.*) What color is it? (*It appears to have no color.*) Do you know what will happen if I put this crystal in sunlight (or shine a light through it)? (*If direct sunlight shines nearby, use it. If not, shine a flashlight through the crystal so that a rainbow is produced.*) What do you see?

I think crystals are fun to have. *On a sunny window at my house, I have something that looks like an owl, made of brass, sitting on a tree branch. Where the owl's eyes and stomach should be, there are crystals. When the sun shines through the crystals, it makes rainbows in the room. I showed the rainbows to my little grandson one day. He tried to pick a rainbow off the wall. Then I let the rainbow shine on his hand. He was puzzled. He didn't understand why he couldn't take the rainbow with him.

Another day, my husband saw a spot on the carpet. The carpet is a dark-gold color. So he saw only a burnt orange color, not all of the rainbow's colors. He thought the dark spot was a stain from something spilled onto the floor. He got a damp cloth and tried to wipe up the spot, but no matter how hard he tried, he couldn't wipe it up.

One afternoon, my Christian writers' group gathered around the table. We were helping one another with our writing. Suddenly one said, "There's a rainbow on your wall!" She was excited to see it. I showed her that there were six rainbows in all in different parts of the room.

Do you know how it happens that this crystal makes rainbows? Ordinary sunlight has all the colors of the rainbow in it. We don't see the colors because they are blended together. The crystal breaks up the sunlight and lets us see the colors.

Have you ever heard someone say, "It's crystal clear" or, "It's clear as crystal"? That usually means the person sees or understands something well, just as crystal lets light shine through it. But if someone says, "It's clear as mud," what do you think that means? The person doesn't see or understand something. It's the opposite of "clear as crystal." Mud doesn't let light shine through it.

There are many places in the Bible where we can read about light. One place is in a letter that the apostle Paul wrote to the Christians at Corinth: "For it is the God who said, 'Let light shine out of darkness,' who has shone in our hearts to give light of the knowledge of the glory of God in the face of Jesus Christ" (2 Corinthians 4:6). Paul means that it is our task—our job—to let people see God through us. We can let God's light shine in our hearts so we can give that light— what we know about Jesus and God's love—to others.

I'm going to tell you about some things that could happen to you. Your part is to think about it and decide yes or no. Am I letting people see God through me?

1. I accidentally bumped Susan's tray. Her soup spilled all over her tray. I said I was sorry and I helped her to clean up the mess. I gave her my soup. Yes or no? Am I letting people see God through me? (*Allow enough time for children to decide.*) Why do you think so?

2. Sometimes Ann wears dirty clothes that are too small for her. On other days, she wears her brother's shirts that are too big for her. I told my friends, "Let's not play with her." What could I do that might let people see God through me?

3. I had two candy bars on my desk. I went out to play. When I came back, only one candy bar was there. Jimmy said that he saw

Bryan eating a candy bar like mine. I don't like Bryan anymore. What would Jesus do?

4. I started sneezing at day care (or school). I covered my nose and mouth when I sneezed. I didn't want to give my cold to anyone else. How or why is this letting people see God through me?

5. I was playing a game with my friends. They were way ahead of me. My marker was the last one on the board. I knew I was going to lose. When no one was looking, I moved my marker closer to the finish line. Why isn't this letting people see God through me?

6. My brother took my bike without asking me if he could. He hit a pole and banged up my bike. I was angry! He said he was sorry and promised he would ask me the next time. He's going to fix my bike. I forgave him. How is this like God?

Letting people see God through you means that you do what is right, fair, true, honest, kind, loving, and forgiving of others. That is what God does.

When you let God shine through you, you turn sunshine into a rainbow! You can do it with a smile or a kind word. You can do it by holding a door open for someone or helping to carry a heavy load. You can do it by telling someone what you know about Jesus.

When you see sunlight shining through a crystal, a prism, or raindrops, let it remind you to let the love of God shine through you. Something beautiful will come of it.

OPTIONAL: STRETCHING FURTHER
(Read aloud Matthew 5:14–16: "You are the light of the world.") How brightly are you shining—showing others what God and Christ are like? like a 150-watt bulb? like a night-light? How can we help one another to shine brighter?

Let's pray. (Ask children to bow their heads and repeat after you. Say short, meaningful phrases.)

Dear God, thank you for the beautiful colors in sunlight and the rainbow. Thank you for letting your light shine in my heart. Help me to show your love as clear as crystal to others. In Jesus' name. Amen.

23
Claiming Territory

THEME: God created the world and all that is in it. We need to share it with one another.

SCRIPTURE: The heavens are yours, the earth also is yours; the world and all that is in it—you have founded them.—Psalm 89:11

PREPARATION: Make a sign with a dark marker on tagboard or poster paper, at least 8 1/2" x 11", saying, "No Trespassing."

---

*Have you seen a robin lately? I've noticed that the birds that go someplace where it's warmer in winter have come back. Did you know that, when winter is almost over, the male birds fly north before the females do? Why do you think they do that? The males fly north early because they need to claim a territory—a place where they and their mates can build nests and find enough food for themselves and their baby birds.

What happens when too many birds claim the same territory—trees, bushes, lawns, or fields? They fight, fly at each other, and peck one another until one bird drives the other away. If too many birds are in the same area, there won't be enough food for all of them.

Can you think of other animals that claim their territory? Deer keep to their own patch of forest. They have special glands under the eyes, on the forehead, and in the clefts of their hoofs. Those glands make smelly fluids that the deer rub on the ground and on twigs and branches to mark the edges of their territory. The smell tells other deer that this patch of forest is already claimed.

Do you know how black bears mark their territory? They make claw and tooth marks on trees in their area.

What about people? Do we mark our territory, too? How? We lock our doors. People put up fences and walls. We plant bushes and hedges to separate our "territory" from our neighbor's place. Have you ever seen a sign like this? *(Display "No Trespassing" sign.)* Hunters sometimes see signs like this on land where they would like to hunt. Do you know what it means? It means keep off; if you don't keep off, you will have to pay a fine.

*I've noticed that people claim their territory inside, too. At the indoor pool where I swim, each person chooses a lane that is set apart by a cable from the other lanes. If lots of people come to swim at the same time, they have to share lanes. If too many swimmers are in the pool at the same time, it's hard to stay in a lane without bumping into another swimmer. People become annoyed and unhappy when that happens.

What about where you live? Is there a special place that is yours, and you don't want anyone else to be there? *(Suggest a room, part of a room, toy area, or a chair at table.)*

Let's think about our church building(s). Do we claim our special territory here, too? We might try to park our car always in the same spot. Maybe we hang our coats in the same part of the coat rack every Sunday. Many of us make it a habit always to sit in the same pew or in the same part of the room where we worship.

Is it good to make habits like that? It can be good in some ways. People who know you and need to talk to you always know where to look for you. If your car or your coat is always in the same place, it's not hard to remember where it is.

Is there anything wrong with feeling that you *own* a certain place, and no one else may have it or use it? That's selfish, isn't it? Thinking only about yourself and no one else?

What could you do if you come into church or Sunday school and find someone else in the place that is usually yours? If it's someone you don't know, maybe you could say something like, "Hi, I'm Ginny. May I sit beside you?" Get to know that person and learn to enjoy worshiping or working with him or her.

What about God? Does God claim or mark territory that is God's, and only God's? *(If so, ask where, what, and how big God's territory is.)* Is this church building God's territory?

Let's hear what the Bible says about God's territory. In the first verse of the first book in the Bible, Genesis, we read: "In the beginning when God created the heavens and the earth." In Psalm 89:11, the writer says to God, "The heavens are yours, the earth also is yours; the world and all that is in it—you have founded them." God made the world and everything in it. Let's name some things that God created. *(You may want to use the words of "All Things Bright and Beautiful" by Cecil Frances Alexander as a guide or starting point.)* In the first book of Genesis, verse 31, we read: "God saw everything that he had made, and indeed, it was very good."

It's all God's territory, isn't it? We need to remember, especially when we are claiming a special spot as *our* territory, that it really belongs to God.

God made all of us, too. God gave all people a special part in the earth God created. God wants us to live in peace with other people. Jesus said, "Blessed are the peacemakers, for they will be called children of God" (Matthew 5:9). We have peace only when we are kind and loving toward other people, and sharing—not being selfish—God's territory.

I hope that you can take some time today or tomorrow to go for a walk. Invite a friend or a family member to walk with you. Walk slowly. Take deep breaths. Look for things that God has created. Find something small to bring back with you that reminds you of God and all that God has created for us to enjoy. It might be a leaf, a twig, a flower, or a pebble. Put it in a place where you will see it this week. Thank God for God's creation, and live in peace with everyone with whom you share God's territory.

OPTIONAL: STRETCHING FURTHER
We call the church building God's "house." Why? When we leave here, does God leave, too?

Let's pray. *(Ask children to bow their heads and repeat after you. Say short, meaningful phrases.)*

Dear God, you are so good. Thank you for the beautiful world you made. Help us to share your territory and to love all people everywhere. In Jesus' name. Amen.

24
Putting Things in Order

THEME: God brings order out of chaos.

SCRIPTURE: In the beginning when God created the heavens and the earth, the earth was a formless void and darkness covered the face of the deep, while a wind from God swept over the face of the waters.—Genesis 1:1–2

PREPARATION: Stuff your pockets or purse with an assortment of odds and ends, including humorous, unlikely items. Be prepared to empty your pockets or pocketbook as you pretend to hunt for a missing car or house key.

Hello, girls and boys. *Will you excuse me for a few minutes? I have a problem. (*Rummage through purse or pockets.*) I don't know where my car key is. I thought I put it in my purse, but I can't find it. If I can't find it, I don't know how I will go home after church. I hope I didn't lock it inside my car. That would be really embarrassing because I'd have to find a police officer and ask for help to open my locked car door. I just can't find my key in my pocketbook!

Can you help me? What should I do? Do you think I should just take *everything* out of my bag? (*Dump entire contents of bag on the floor near you. Make comments about finding other items you've been hunting for such as stamps, a film-lab or dry-cleaning ticket, a "things to do" list, sunglasses, swim cap, prayer request, or get well card.*) Who's good at finding things?

(*After a child near you finds the key.*) There it is! Phew! (*Wipe brow.*) Thank you for helping me to find my key. I'm so glad that I *did* put it in my pocketbook after all. But I'm embarrassed about all the *stuff* we had to sort through before we found what we were hunting for.

Do you have anything that is as messy or cluttered as my bag? Do you have a bag or backpack that you take along when you go to visit someone, or go to day care or to school? Can you always find what you're looking for in it? What about a toy box or the room where you play? Are your things in order, or are they just in a pile or scattered about the room?

How do you feel when you can't find what you need? It's not a good feeling when that happens to me. If you go to school, your teacher expects you to bring certain papers to school. Your teacher will be unhappy if you don't bring the papers you're supposed to bring. Maybe you need to take your lunch or some money to buy lunch. You will be very unhappy if you don't have lunch, won't you?

When I'm unhappy, I like to hear what God says to me. Do you think we can find anything in the Bible that will help us with finding things we need? I'm going to look in the very beginning of the Bible—in the book of Genesis. *(Read Genesis 1:1–2.)*

Those words didn't say anything about pocketbooks or backpacks or toy boxes, did they? Listen again: "In the beginning . . . God created the heavens and the earth." Who made the heavens and the earth? Yes, God made the heavens and the earth. Listen again: "The earth was a formless void." That means there was just empty space. There was no shape or order to anything. From *nothing*, God made the heavens and the earth. What else did God make? *(Light, day, night, sky, oceans, dry land, plants, stars, sun, moon, animals, people.)*

God made a wonderful universe, and God made it well. The earth we live on is part of a huge group of stars called a "galaxy" that spins at 490,000 miles an hour. It takes 200 million years for this galaxy we live in to make one rotation or turn. There are more than one billion other galaxies like ours in this huge, immense universe that God made. Some scientists say that the number of stars in creation is as many as all the grains of sand on all the beaches of the world. Yet, this whole, complicated system of spinning stars works well, just as God made it to do.

It works well because God made order out of a mess. God is a God of order, not disorder or clutter, like my pocketbook. God made night to come after day, and we count on day to come after night. What season do we expect to come after summer? After fall, or autumn, what season do we expect? after winter? after spring? The seasons always come in the same order, according to God's plan.

What if you planted a potato and up came an elephant? That isn't the way God planned it, is it?

Have you ever dropped some food while you were eating? Where did the food land? What if you dropped mashed potatoes and they fell up and stuck to the ceiling instead of the floor? God's laws always work just as God planned. One of those laws is God's law of gravity that makes things fall down instead of up.

"Neat" is a word that means the opposite of cluttered, jumbled, mixed-up and disordered. I couldn't find the word "neat" in my Bible, but I did find this: "God is a God not of disorder but of peace" (1 Corinthians 14:33). We are to become more and more like God. So we should want to put things in order, too. And when there is order, there is also peace. If your toys and clothes are in order and where they belong, Mom and Dad won't have to nag you!

For some of us, it's a hard job to put things in order; for others it's not so hard. We can put things in order in many different ways. Let's think about toys. Can you think of a way that you could put your toys or toy box in order? (By *size, color, how often you use them.*) Could you have one place to put books, another place for stuffed animals, and another for board games?

This week, think about something or someplace that you can put in order. You might ask your parents to help you. Maybe you will want to put your bag or backpack in order in the evening for the next day. Keeping things in order helps us to make better use of the time God has given us, too, because we won't have to waste a lot of time hunting for important things. Planning ahead helps us keep things in order.

I know what I'm going to do as soon as I go back home. I'm going to empty my pocketbook again and put things where they belong—where I can find them. The next place I need to put in order is my workroom—the place where I study and write. That's going to be a *big* job!

Remember, too, that no matter how bad things may seem, no matter how mixed-up or messed up things may seem, God has a plan. God has a plan for *you*. God loves you and wants to use you in that plan. God wants the best for us. We should want to learn more of God's plans for us each day.

OPTIONAL: STRETCHING FURTHER

The word "Genesis" means "beginnings." Where or how will you make a new beginning? (*Beginning a new calendar or school year; beginning vacation or summer Bible school; beginning a year as a six-year-old.*) Who will help you to put things in order for your new beginning? How can you help?

Let's pray. (*Ask children to bow their heads and repeat after you. Say short, meaningful phrases.*)

Dear God, thank you for the universe that you made. You are awesome! We want to be more like you. Help us to learn how to put things in good order. Help us to fit into your plan for us. We pray in Jesus' name. Amen.

25

God Knows Your Name

THEME: God knows your name. God will not forget you.

SCRIPTURE: I will not forget you. See, I have inscribed you on the palms of my hands.—Isaiah 49:15b–16

PREPARATION: Obtain a set of plastic or magnetic letters and board, a small chalkboard and chalk, or a marker board and marker. Also bring an identification bracelet or a shirt or cap with the name of a person or team on it. A birth certificate and a family Bible with names written inside are also appropriate for showing and sharing.

Hello, boys and girls. Let's talk about names today. My name is *(your name)*. Some of you already knew my name, didn't you? I know some of your names, too, but not everyone's name. *(Invite every child to say her or his name. Give a special welcome to visitors.)* Have you ever been in a place with a lot of people and no one knew your name? How did that make you feel? Did you want someone to know you or talk to you or notice you?

Do we need names? If we want to say something to someone, can't we just say, "Hey! You!"? No, that wouldn't be friendly or polite, would it?

We need names to identify ourselves to other people—to tell one person from another. Have you ever been in a group or class where there was another person with the same name as yours? Some names are more popular than others. Have you ever been in a group where there was more than one James? *(Place or print "James" twice on a marker board, magnetic board, flannel board, or chalkboard.)* How can you, your classmates, and your teacher let each James know which one you're talking to? You can use last names or initials. James Hoover could be called "James H."; James Smith could be called "James S." *(Add "H." and "S." to the names.)*

Names are important. From the moment we are born, we are given some kind of label or name. *I brought a tiny bracelet of blue and white beads to show you. It was put on my son's arm right after he was born. We hadn't given him a name yet, so the name on the bracelet is my last name—our family name. Because of the bracelet on his arm, we were always sure we had *our* baby and not a baby belonging to someone else.

Names are written for many different reasons. Where have you seen your name written? *(In a playgroup, class list, day care list, sports team, Bible school, on a birthday card, on your clothes, on a package or gift.)* Here is another way we show that your name is important. *(Show birth certificate.)* When you or your parents need to show how old you are, like the time when you start going to school, this certificate tells when you were born, as well as who you are.

Another special place to write your name and birth date is in a family Bible. Long before birth certificates, Bibles were the place to write information about births and deaths, too. *(Show.)*

Do you think your name is important to God? Why? (or why not?) Let's see what the Bible—God's Word—says. In the book of Isaiah, we read about a time long ago—almost 600 years before Jesus was born. The city of Jerusalem had been destroyed by enemies of Israel, and the people had been captured and taken away to live in a place called Babylon. The temple in Jerusalem had also been destroyed. Some people wondered if God was strong enough to help them. They thought God might even forget about them.

Listen to what the Lord said to the people through Isaiah: "I will not forget you. See, I have inscribed you on the palms of my hands" (Isaiah 49:15b–16). God could not possibly forget Israel because God is like a loving mother to them. God meant, "I wrote your name on the palms of my hands so that whenever I lift up my hands or open them, I'll see your name and remember you." And God keeps promises. Many years later God led the people of Israel to return and rebuild Jerusalem.

In the part of the Bible that tells about Jesus and his disciples, we read a letter that the apostle Paul wrote to Timothy. Paul wrote, "The Lord knows those who are his" (2 Timothy 2:19). We belong to God. God knows *our* names, too. God won't forget us.

In the Gospel of Luke, we read about a time when Jesus sent seventy of his followers out to heal those who were sick and to say: "The kingdom of God has come near" (10:9). When the seventy came back, they were excited and happy about what they had done. But Jesus said, "Do not rejoice at this . . . but rejoice that your names are written in heaven" (10:20). Of all the wonders that God works, the greatest wonder of all is that *we* can be citizens of heaven. When we trust in Jesus, our names our written there.

Here is another wonder. In the last book of the Bible—the Revelation—we read about Jesus' apostle John. God sent an angel to show John what will happen in the future. The angel said, "To everyone who conquers . . . I will give a white stone, and on the white stone is written a new name that no one knows except the one who receives it" (Revelation 2:17). When we die and go to be with Jesus, everything will be new. We will have a new home, a new body, a new life, and a new name. You are so important to God that God has reserved a new, special name just for you.

But while we are living here on earth, the most important name for us to know is . . . (*Change the name of "James" to "Jesus."*) . . . Jesus. Why do you think it's so important for us to know Jesus? Jesus shows us how to become God's children. Whoever believes in Jesus can be forgiven for doing wrong things, and can live in heaven with him forever.

Do you all know how to write your name? If you haven't learned to do that yet, you might want to ask someone who's older to help you to learn this week. Here's another name for you to learn to write. (*Indicate "Jesus."*) Let's say the names of the letters that spell "Jesus." (*Say the letters slowly with the children several times.*) Now let's close our eyes and spell "Jesus." Good! I hope you will keep on practicing spelling and writing the name of Jesus. Every time you say or write his name, remember, too, that Jesus loves you and he knows your name, too.

OPTIONAL: STRETCHING FURTHER

Talk about other names by which Christ is called, (see Revelation 19:16), such as "Faithful and True," "The Word of God," "King of kings and Lord of lords." Emphasize that no name can do Jesus justice. He is greater than any description or expression the human mind can devise.

Let's pray. (*Ask children to bow their heads and repeat after you. Say short, meaningful phrases.*)

Dear God, thank you for loving us. You loved us so much that you sent us Jesus. We are glad that you know our names. Help us to love one another, as Jesus shows us how. We pray in his precious name. Amen.

26
Jesus Brings Good News

THEME: The gospel is good news.

SCRIPTURE: For God so loved the world that he gave his only Son, so that everyone who believes in him may not perish but may have eternal life.—John 3:16

PREPARATION: 1.) Gather various sources of news: newspaper, magazine, church bulletin or newsletter, magazine, e-mailed or faxed letter, small radio, or a report card. A canvas bag would be an appropriate container for them; 2.) Print or type the words of John 3:16 on paper or tagboard strips to be copied and cut apart as bookmarks, about 2 1/2" x 8 1/2". (An alternative might be to purchase commercially made bookmarks or stickers stating this scripture.); 3.) An optional visual aid can be a long sheet of freezer paper, wax paper, or paper towels attached to two cylindrical cardboard tubes to simulate a scroll.

(Hand out, or let children reach into the bag and take out one item apiece. Let each child try to tell what he or she has chosen. Help to identify the items if necessary.) Look around at all the things that were in the bag. Do you know any way in which these things are all alike? They all tell us something we may not have known before. We can learn news from all of these articles. There are other ways we can find out what's happening, too, but I couldn't fit them into this bag. Can you think of other ways to learn news? *(Television, Internet, word of mouth.)*

Today we are talking about news. *When I was a teenager, I delivered a weekly newspaper to people in the small town where I lived. I didn't mind delivering the newspaper when I knew there was good news in it, because I knew the good news would make people happy. They liked to read about their favorite ball team winning a game, people getting engaged and married, babies being born, or young people graduating from high school or college. But I didn't like delivering bad news about people being sick, being hurt in accidents, and having homes and businesses damaged by hurricanes, fires, and floods. Bad news made people feel sad.

When I was in high school, I delivered news in another way, too. I delivered mail to about twenty-five families in my neighborhood. Every morning before school, I rode my bike to the post office, picked up a canvas bag with the mail in it, and rode back to my house. There, I spread the mail out on the dining room floor and put it in order according to where the people lived. Then, on my way to school, I stopped at each house, put the mail in a mailbox near the door, or slipped it between the door and the screen door, and called out, "Mail!" I did the same thing again after school! In those days, people received mail twice a day. And for delivering their mail, each family gave me what they could afford—from twenty-five cents a month to two dollars. Many of them gave me gifts at Christmastime, too.

That was long ago, but even longer ago, when Jesus lived on Earth, there were no newspapers, radios, television sets, computers, trains, airplanes, or cars to bring us news. People learned what was happening mostly by listening to someone telling it. They did have some stories written on scrolls—like big rolls of paper—to help them remember what happened long ago.

In the book of Luke, we read about Jesus in a place called Nazareth. Jesus was just beginning to teach in the synagogues—the places where the people worshiped God. (*Read aloud Luke 4:16–21.*) When we turn toward the beginning of the Bible, we find the book of Isaiah. In Isaiah 61:1–2, we can read the same message that Jesus read, but in a different language. Seven hundred years before Jesus was born, God had shown Isaiah that Jesus would be born to live and die on earth. Isn't that amazing?

Jesus read the scroll of Isaiah and told the people "Today this scripture has been fulfilled in your hearing" (Luke 4:21). Jesus is saying, "I am the one Isaiah wrote about. This scripture has come true today. I bring good news. I *am* the good news."

Another word that means good news is "gospel." The gospel is meant to make glad the people who hear it. Jesus brought hope to the people. God sent Jesus as a gift to everyone and especially to those who were poor, hurting, and sad. The gospel is more than one message or thing that Jesus did. Jesus Christ *is* the gospel. In the book of John we read, "For God so loved the world that he gave his only Son, so that everyone who believes in him may not perish but may have eternal life" (John 3:16). This is one of the most famous verses in the Bible. It means we will die, but if we believe in Jesus, we will live again. We will live forever with him. That's what "eternal life" means. That is the good news!

After Jesus died and God brought him to life again, Jesus sent the disciples to tell the good news. They traveled and spoke about Jesus to many people. When they wrote about Jesus to help people learn about God, the writings of Matthew, Mark, Luke, and John were called the Gospels.

I have a bookmark for each of you. On it are the words of the gospel—the good news. (*Read John 3:16.*) We have many ways to learn and give news today. This message is one that you can share with your friends and neighbors. You can bring good news to people who don't know it.

Optional: Stretching Further

Read aloud Matthew 28:18–20 and talk about what Jesus told his disciples to do. Note that in Matthew 10:5–6, Jesus had sent his disciples only to the Jews. From now on, they should tell the good news throughout the world. Jesus died for the sins of people from *all* nations, not only the Jews.

Let's pray. (*Ask children to bow their heads and repeat after you. Say short, meaningful phrases.*)

Dear God, thank you for loving us so much that you gave us your son, Jesus. Help us to tell the good news to those who don't know it. We pray in Jesus' name. Amen.

Bibliography

ABC's of the Bible. Pleasantville, N.Y.: Reader's Digest Association, 1991.

Fisher, Dorothy Canfield. *What Shall We Do Now? Over Five Hundred Games and Pastimes: A Book of Suggestions for Children's Games and Employments.* New York: Frederick A. Stokes, 1922.

Hall, Godfrey. *Games.* New York: Thomson Learning, 1995.

Hindman, Darwin Alexander. *Complete Book of Games and Stunts.* Englewood Cliffs, N.J.: Prentice-Hall, 1956.

Holy Bible: International Children's Bible. New Century Version. Dallas, Tex: Word, 1988.

Life Application Bible: New International Version. Wheaton, Ill.: Tyndale House; Grand Rapids, Mich.: Zondervan, 1991.

National Council of the Churches of Christ in the United States of America. The Holy Bible: New Revised Standard Version Bible. Grand Rapids, Mich.: Zondervan, 1989.

Osborne, Rick. *Talking to Your Children about God.* San Francisco: HarperSanFrancisco, 1998.

The New Book of Knowledge. Danbury, Conn.: Grolier, 1994.

Weiser, Franz Xavier. *Handbook of Christian Feasts and Customs: The Year of the Lord in Liturgy and Folklore.* New York: Harcourt, Brace, 1958.

Index

Advent, 11, 13, 15, 18

Andrew, 28

angels, 18, 53, 84

animals, 53, 57, 77

Bible, 50, 53, 57, 60, 63, 84, 88

child of God, 13, 23, 44

Christmas, 15, 18

circles, 13, 63

clothes, 63

Creator, 66, 77, 80

David, 47

disciples, 28, 41, 53, 88

doubt, 53

Easter, 37, 47, 50, 53

fasting, 37

fish, 28

food, 13, 23, 28, 37

forgiveness, 47, 57

games, 70

Gethsemane, 41

gifts, 15, 26

God's love, 13, 31

good news, 18, 50, 88

gospel, 88

growing, 34, 66

heaven, 84

honor, 21

James, 28

Jesus' birth, 11

John, 28, 84

Joseph, 11, 34

joy, 15, 50

kneeling, 21

Lent, 37, 41, 44, 47

light, 60, 74

listen, 44

look, 44

love, 13, 31, 44, 57

Mary, 11, 13, 23, 50

Mary Magdalene, 50, 53

messages, 50

miracles, 23, 28

music, 63

names, 11, 63, 84

Nazareth, 88

order, 80

Paul, 15, 34, 47, 60, 63, 66, 84

Peter, 41

Pilate, 44

planting, 66

praying, 21, 37, 41

rainbow, 74

recipe, 66

respect, 21

Savior, 11

seasons, 18

seeds, 66

servants, 44, 66

signs, 23

Simon, 28

sin, 47

spring, 66

stealing, 47

symbols, 28

temptations, 41

Thomas, 53

treasures, 57

trees, 18

valentines, 31

winter, 18

wisdom, 57

wise men, 21

witnesses, 53

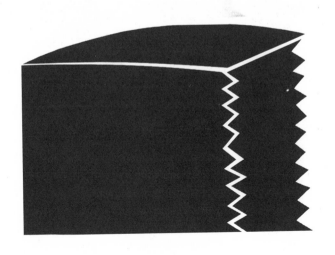

OTHER BOOKS FROM THE PILGRIM PRESS

Adult worship services can be uplifting and inspiring for adults, but difficult for children. Our collection of children's sermons ensures that worship can be uplifting and inspiring for the young. Choose from among our selection of children's sermons that include the lectionary-based *Time with Our Children*, the smorgasbord of age-appropriate messages presented by *The Brown Bag*, or the celebration of children in *Small Wonders*.

THE BROWN BAG
Jerry Marshall Jordan
ISBN 0-8298-0411-0/paper/117 pages/$9.95

SMALL WONDERS
Sermons for Children
Glen E. Rainsley
ISBN 0-8298-1252-0/paper/104 pages/$12.95

TIME WITH OUR CHILDREN
Stories for Use in Worship, Year B
Dianne E. Deming
ISBN 0-8298-0952-X/paper/182 pages/$9.95

TIME WITH OUR CHILDREN
Stories for Use in Worship, Year C
Dianne E. Deming
ISBN 0-8298-0953-8/paper/157 pages/$9.95

To order these or any other books from The Pilgrim Press call or write to:
The Pilgrim Press
700 Prospect Avenue East
Cleveland, Ohio 44115-1100

Phone orders: 800.537.3394
Fax orders: 216.736.2206
Please include shipping charges of $4.00 for the first book and
75¢ for each additional book.
Or order from our Web sites at
www.pilgrimpress.com and www.ucpress.com.

Prices subject to change without notice.